PLUNGING

THROUGH

THE CLOUDS

PLUNGING

THROUGH

THE CLOUDS

Constructive Living Currents

Edited by

David K. Reynolds

State University of New York Press

Production: Ruth Fisher
Marketing: Dana E. Yanulavich

Published by
State University of New York Press, Albany

For information, address State University of New York Press,
State University Plaza, Albany, N.Y., 12246

Library of Congress Cataloging-in-Publication Data

Plunging through the clouds : constructive living currents / edited by
   David K. Reynolds.
      p.   cm.
   Includes bibliographical references (p.   ) and index.
   ISBN 0-7914-1313-6 (acid-free). — ISBN 0-7914-1314-4 (pbk. : acid
-free)
   1. Morita psychotherapy.   2. Naikan psychotherapy.   I. Reynolds,
David K.
   RC489.M65P58   1993
   616.89'14—dc20   91-45686
                                                          CIP

10 9 8 7 6 5 4 3 2 1

CONTENTS

Preface   ix

Acknowledgments   xi

INTRODUCTION

1. Overview
   David K. Reynolds   3

2. Morita and Naikan Therapies—Similarities
   David K. Reynolds   11

3. The Water Books
   David K. Reynolds   21

4. Constructive Living for the Well—Toward a
   Superior Life
   Patricia Ryan Madson   29

5. Constructive Living, A First Look
   Rami M. Shapiro   35

CONSTRUCTIVE LIVING AND SOCIETY

6. Constructive Living and Morita Therapy: Some
   Possible Applications to Child Rearing
   Mary J. Puckett   51

7. Constructive Living for High School Students
   Barbara Sarah and Perri Ardman   63

8. Morita's Principles and HIV Infection
   Gregory Willms   69

9. Exploring Group Models for Teaching The
    Principles of Constructive Living
            Gregg Krech   75

CONSTRUCTIVE LIVING AND BUSINESS

10. Constructive Living and Business
            Mary J. Puckett   87

11. Doing a Good Job: Constructive Living
    Guidelines for Life at Work
            Gregg Krech   93

CONSTRUCTIVE LIVING AND REFLECTION

Introduction to Naikan   105

12. The Practice of Naikan
            Gregg Krech   109

13. Shidosha
            Patricia Ryan Madson   121

14. Constructive Living Correspondence
            Patricia Ryan Madson
            Gregory Willms
            Michael Whiteley
            Marilyn Murray   131

15. Reflections on Reflection
            Susan Jensen Kahn   141

PERSONAL EXPERIENCES WITH
CONSTRUCTIVE LIVING

16. Just Doing It
            Lynn Sanae Reynolds   147

17. Personal Experience with Morita Guidance
        Henry Kahn   153

18. Constructive Living—Its Benefits
        Michael Whiteley   157

19. Year-End Letter
        Barbara Sarah   161

20. Some Comments on My Experience with
     Constructive Living
        Jim Hutchinson   165

HISTORICAL BACKGROUND

21. Morita Masatake: The Life of the Founder
     of Morita Therapy
        David K. Reynolds   169

22. Yoshimoto Ishin: The Life of the Founder
     of Naikan
        David K. Reynolds   173

References   **183**

Constructive Living Activities   **187**

Contributors   **191**

Index   **195**

PREFACE

Some 90% of normal students in a psychiatric study had excessive worries and fears about personal relationships, illness, imperfection, stray thoughts, lack of sleep, poor memory, or uncleanliness. (Kora, Seikatsu no Hakken Magazine, 1990, Nr. 4, p. 12) The study was of Japanese students in 1937. People aren't so different across time and cultures, are they? There is no worry-free existence for humans.

The hope of completely eliminating neurotic suffering either by talking or by medication seems pretty much gone, I think. Talking with the aim of developing some magical insight does little more than make self-centered people more self-centered. And medication may relieve some anxiety at the cost of dulled senses, chemical dependency, and unpleasant physical side effects. Moreover, feeling-centered "fixes" merely produce people who are more feeling-focused.

The revolutionary idea that human existence necessarily includes anxiety and suffering isn't a new one, of course. But it has been forgotten by many as science and technology solve so many human problems with understanding and technical sophistication. Constructive Living reminds us of important tasks which present themselves to us whether we are hurting in this moment or not. Even feelings we don't relish—feelings like guilt, fear, timidity, and despair—are natural aspects of our changing circumstances. They may inform but need not determine our actions. Constructive Living may be seen as a way of working around human misery. And it is more than that.

In this book, I have pulled together works by a number of colleagues in Constructive Living. Each has his or her own style of describing and practicing Constructive Living. Some stay closer to the Japanese therapies (Morita therapy and Naikan) upon which many of the fundamental ideas of Constructive

Living are based. Others range further from the roots in order to offer principles and practices more acceptable to Westerners. This variety of wording and overall presentation and adaptation demonstrates the breadth of Constructive Living. I consider all of the varieties presented here valid and useful. It is unimportant to preserve an orthodoxy, but it is vitally important to adapt in order to meet the needs of individual Constructive Living students.

The title of this book comes from a strong image in Natsume Soseki's book, *The Miner.* Striding up a mountain, pushing through the clouds—it is often what life seems to be about.

ACKNOWLEDGMENTS

This book, too, is borrowed. It is the product of the efforts put forth by Constructive Living contributors, by William Eastman and his staff at SUNY Press, by those who fed and taught us. Naikan reflection reminds us that the list of those who support and sustain our work is without end.

My activities in Japan were supported, in part, by the Mental Health Okamoto Memorial Foundation.

INTRODUCTION

1

OVERVIEW

DAVID K. REYNOLDS

ABOUT CONSTRUCTIVE LIVING

Constructive Living (an extension of the Japanese Morita and Naikan psychotherapies) is becoming increasingly well-known in academic literature and the popular press in the West. Wiley's *Encyclopedia of Psychology* contains entries for Morita and Naikan therapies. The best-selling college introductory psychology textbook, *Psychology and Life*, written by Zimbardo at Stanford devotes nearly a page to Morita therapy. The *Handbook of Innovative Psychotherapies* contains chapters on Morita therapy and on Naikan therapy. Articles about Morita therapy have appeared in *Psychiatric Quarterly, Psychotherapy, Journal of Counseling and Development,* and other academic journals. Book reviews of Constructive Living books have appeared in *JAMA, Psychology Today, Contemporary Psychology,* and elsewhere. The *International Bulletin of Morita Therapy* is published at the Department of Counselling Psychology of the University of British Columbia.

As for the popular press, the May, 1990, silver anniversary issue of *Cosmopolitan* carried a long article about Constructive Living prompting more than 5,000 readers from every state and a number of foreign countries to write asking for more information. Recent articles also appeared in *USA Today* (August

23, 1990), *Bottom Line* (December 11, 1990, pp. 11–12), *Your Personal Best* (Charter issue), *New Dimensions* (May–June, 1990, pp. 29–30), and *American Health* (March, 1991, p. 12). The November, 1991, issue of *New Woman* magazine featured a lengthy article on Constructive Living.

WHAT IS CONSTRUCTIVE LIVING?

Constructive Living follows an educational, not a medical model. The goal of Constructive Living (CL) is to help students learn to become more "realistic." Neurotic problems seem to have their roots and expression in a sort of unrealistic approach to life. Unfortunately, traditional psychodynamic Western psychotherapy offers little toward developing a broader perspective on reality. For example, in traditional counseling modes, the typical suffering students focus much attention on the reality of inner feeling states and miss much of the varied and vital situational reality surrounding them. Western therapy repeatedly focuses attention on internal states promoting little concern with observation of external reality and behavioral objectives prompted by that reality. Similarly, Western therapy tends to emphasize the negative aspects of parenting (thus conveniently excusing the client's responsibility for current problem behavior) while ignoring the sacrifices and service of (admittedly imperfect) parental figures. The action (Morita) and reflection (Naikan) aspects of Constructive Living redirect the students' attention toward those parts of reality which have been systematically ignored or dismissed in the West.

Morita and Naikan therapies are practiced separately by a variety of therapists in Japan. Morita psychotherapy is practiced primarily as a medical sub-specialty within the field of psychiatry. Naikan has a wider range of practitioners and settings and covers a broader range of client complaints. Both methods are based on careful observation and intense introspection by their founders—Morita Masatake (or Morita Shoma) and Yoshimoto Ishin (Japanese family names precede the given names). My functions were to contribute to the introduction of these methods to the West; to point out the philosophical and methodological complementarity of the two to Easterners and

Westerners; and to extend the theories, methods, and applications beyond their narrow ranges in Japan. Constructive Living is a thoroughly Western therapeutic approach to living now. Its methods are increasingly adopted back into Japan as that country becomes more Westernized. Innovations in method are exchanged as I continue to lecture and present papers about CL in Japanese at the national and international Morita and Naikan meetings in Japan each year. We are in the process of repaying our debt to our mentors, although the debt keeps growing.

Introductory material on Morita therapy and Naikan therapy may be found in Reynolds, 1976, 1980, 1983, 1989, 1990, and 1991.

The Action Aspect of Constructive Living

Briefly, Morita therapy recommends the sensible life strategy of accepting uncontrollable aspects of life (such as feelings, other people, weather, outcomes of actions, and the like) while using energy and effort to affect that single element of life which we control directly, our behavior. This action element of CL prompts a minimum of talk during CL instruction and puts a premium on homework assignments to be carried out by the student. These assignments provide the student with experiential understanding of the effectiveness of constructive action in changing an unrealistic life style. Students learn that it is unnecessary to "fix" feelings or become "comfortable" with an activity before undertaking it. No multi-step process needs to proceed action—they simply do it.

Feelings may change as a result of positive activity, but such change is only a welcome by-product, not the goal of instruction. The student learns to personally assess situations and do what needs doing simply because it needs doing, not for some desired decrease in anxiety or anticipated increase in self-esteem.

Advanced students of Constructive Living come to accept themselves as part of the reality in which they find themselves. Such a perspective is not passive fatalism; rather, it provokes an active interplay between real circumstances and realistic action aimed at affecting those circumstances.

Morita therapy has a long and respected history in Japan, but it is only recently showing a growth in popularity there. The Japanese Moritist professional organization has more than doubled its membership over the last few years to more than 500 members. And the Moritist lay person organization, Seikatsu no Hakken Kai, has more than 6,000 members and well over a hundred chapters throughout the country.

The Reflection Aspect of Constructive Living

Naikan therapy asks us to reflect on the reality of our past and present life. Naikan suggests that we examine critically those commonly held views: we have struggled to overcome the obstacles others have placed in our paths; we have succeeded, thanks to our own efforts; we are givers and not takers from the world; we rarely get the rewards we deserve. Such a perspective is unrealistic and is unsupported by consideration of our everyday existence.

Naikan offers methods by which we reflect on our past and on our current situation to gain a more accurate, authentic view of our condition. The exercises recommended in a Naikan approach to mental health invite us to look at our situations from others' points of view, not just from our own self-centered perspective. For example, CL students may be invited to estimate the amount of money their parents spent on them from birth to age twenty-one, then to estimate the amount they spent on their parents during the same period. Similar calculations are made from age twenty-one to the present or until the parents died. Of course, out of pocket expenses are not all there are to relationships, but they provide an objective, measurable scale for comparison of what was given and received materially during childhood and adulthood.

Naikan encourages us to explore the detailed ways in which the world has been supporting us even though we didn't notice the support, didn't thank people and objects for the support, or didn't feel gratitude for it. Beyond what we deserve, we are sustained. Such a realization becomes more than merely an abstract philosophical position when doing Naikan assignments. Sentiments of alienation and anomie generally decline during Naikan.

As a result of Naikan study we learn a substitute for the shaky self-esteem which must be supported by selective forgetting of our failures, our meanness, and others' efforts in our behalf. The substitute is reality esteem. Deserving or not, we continue to be supported by reality. Gratitude and a desire to work at repaying our debt to others replace our greedy endeavors to make sure we get our share.

Naikan is not about forgiving our parents. Such a task is trivial and self-serving. Naikan is about hoping our parents forgive us—for our lack of appreciation of their efforts, for the troubles we caused them, for the little we did for them as we grew up.

As the reader can well imagine, Naikan isn't likely to become popular any time soon in this country. It would be much easier to promote a therapy which sets us up as heroic victims of our pasts and focuses on the inadequacies of our parents. Unfortunately, like the old myth, that psychological insight would cure all our ills, the new myth, that discovering childhood abuse and confronting the abuser will cure our deficits of feeling and behavior, must eventually give way to realistic recognition of Western psychotherapy's essential failure.

When was the last time you saw a neurotic person filled with gratitude? When was the last time you saw a neurotic person bearing a grudge? Narcissistic suffering is neurosis. And most Western psychotherapies seem to operate to make clients even more narcissistic.

THE PRACTICE OF CONSTRUCTIVE LIVING

Instruction in CL consists of individual or group sessions during which the students' attention is directed toward the common reality upon which we all agree, toward realistic behavior based on individual circumstances, and toward reforming existing patterns of behavior and thought. Homework may include reading assignments, cleaning the garage, maintaining a journal of behavior, clipping want ads from the newspaper, writing letters of thanks (whether feeling gratitude or not) to others who served the student in the past, listing goals to be worked toward during the week or month, giving something away each day, observing neighborhood gardens, saying "thank you" ten different ways ten times a day, getting a specified amount of physical exercise, reflection on what was received from and returned to others and troubles caused others during the day, showing up for work regularly, and so forth.

The chapters in this book provide the reader with many concrete examples of CL techniques and goals.

LIMITS OF CONSTRUCTIVE LIVING

Constructive Living is not a psychotherapy for mental illness. Illnesses such as schizophrenia and bipolar disorder require medical care and, usually, some form of psychopharmacological support. Instructors of CL are often mental health professionals, but they are not necessarily so. Constructive Living is an educational program aimed at teaching this effective lifeway to any human who is willing to learn and practice the exercises. Certification in Constructive Living is not a license to practice counseling or psychotherapy.

Certainly, there are people who don't find this lifeway acceptable. They don't come for instruction or they drop out shortly. Other people state their desire to learn but fail to do so. Possible explanations include strong commitment to other ways of seeing the world, low intelligence level, antipathy toward a particular instructor, and unwillingness to put forth the effort required. Compliance is an issue in all forms of directed behavior change, not only in CL.

It is difficult to specify diagnostic categories or personality factors which hinder learning Constructive Living. People are changeable; diagnoses and personality variables are static and fail to reflect the dynamic nature of humans. An individual may be open to learning CL at one time and not at another. At this point in time it is impossible to predict who would successfully undertake and complete a learning course in this method.

ABOUT *PLUNGING THROUGH THE CLOUDS*

This book is the sequel to *Flowing Bridges, Quiet Waters.* It reflects the current status of Constructive Living in the West.

With a couple of exceptions, the contributors to this volume are representatives of the nearly 100 certified instructors (twice that number have received certification training) in the United States and seven foreign countries. Each contributor represents thousands of students who report being helped by CL during its first twelve years of existence in the West.

This book is not a testimonial; it is a status report. The chapters range in style from academic to informal. If the contributions seem unpolished, over-enthusiastic and over-optimistic at times, chalk it up to the early successes of this innovative approach to sensible living. We have seen the excesses of therapies that merely involve self-focused talking. The sheer contrast of CL's method excites hope.

2

MORITA AND NAIKAN THERAPIES—SIMILARITIES

DAVID K. REYNOLDS

THE FOUNDATION FOR FUSION

Morita therapy is reported to be quite effective with phobias, obsessions and panic disorders. Cured and improved rates in the ninetieth percentile are commonly reported. However, certain kinds of students provide difficulties for Morita therapists. Among the difficult students are those who say they have no meaning in life, and that they don't know what needs doing. Other students with interpersonal problems (quarreling with an in-law or with a spouse or with fellow workers, for example) provide similar difficulties. It is not that Morita's method has nothing to offer such students, but it doesn't provide the sort of straightforward, clear advice that it does for a phobia or a panic attack. Some Morita therapists would say simply that Morita doesn't deal with problems of life meaning or interpersonal difficulties. They would argue that Morita therapy is only for treating the neurotic symptoms associated with *shinkeishitsu* neurosis. The *shinkeishitsu* diagnostic category roughly approx-

In slightly different form this chapter was presented as a paper at the First International Congress of Morita Psychotherapy in Hamamatsu, Japan in 1990 and published in Volume 1 Number 2 of the *Journal of Morita Therapy*.

imates obsessive-compulsive disorders, panic disorders, phobic states and neurasthenia. But one cannot define other problems out of existence, and one cannot ignore their existence among people with *shinkeishitsu* diagnoses. How can such people be helped?

Naikan psychotherapy appears to offer just the sort of approach such people need. Naikan is aimed at assisting the student to discover meaning in life and repair damaged interpersonal relationships. Used together in Constructive Living, Morita and Naikan cover most of the presenting problems of the neurotic students we encounter in the West. Of course, I am defining neurotic problems here as non-medical problems. Medical problems involving illness (psychoses, brain lesions, manic-depressive disorder, and the like) require medical treatment beyond the scope of this chapter.

Here I would like to consider some of the similarities between Morita therapy and Naikan therapy that make them complementary and allow them to be used well together in Constructive Living.

Both Morita therapy and Naikan ask the student to look at reality. Morita focuses on the current reality—what needs doing now. Naikan focuses on past reality up to the present. Both emphasize what is realistic and practical. Morita points out that we cannot change our feelings (including our fears and desires) directly by our will, but we can control what we do. Naikan points out that we cannot change the past directly by our will, but we can control our perception of it and attitude toward it.

In a sense, it is unrealistic thinking that is neurosis. Morita therapy emphasizes the unrealistic efforts associated with idealism and perfectionism. Failing to tack down abstract, ideal, theoretical thinking to practical, concrete, specific reality separates the neurotic student from reality. The student tries to do the impossible and so suffers unnecessarily. Naikan therapy emphasizes the unnecessary suffering associated with misperceptions of the past. The neurotic students are oriented toward seeing the faults of others, how much the students gave to others, how little others gave to the students, how much trouble others caused the students. This failure to recognize and remember the concrete, specific support of others in the past, in spite of the trouble the neurotic student caused them, leads to neurotic suffering.

Another element of neurotic suffering which both Morita and Naikan address is that of self-centeredness. The neurotic student is focused inward on misery. Morita points out that this self-focus distracts from attention to the surrounding environment and discovery of what needs doing. Interest is generated by noticing what exists in one's surroundings; interest need not precede the noticing. By losing oneself in one's task or surroundings, neurotic pain disappears. Of course, the purpose of action is not to alleviate pain but to accomplish one's goal. Nevertheless, a side benefit of attention directed away from inner suffering is relief from that suffering.

Naikan points out that extreme concern with getting one's own share results in unnecessary suffering. Why is it that one never encounters a neurotic person who is filled with gratitude? The self-centeredness of neurosis precludes recognition of others' efforts in our behalf. When we recognize that, in spite of our imperfection, we have been supported by our surrounding reality (including people, objects, electricity, and so forth) our neurotic tendencies are diminished. Our focus shifts from self protection to serving others in self sacrifice.

Both Morita and Naikan recognize the naturalness of feelings. Feelings arise naturally from our circumstances and our attitudes toward our circumstances. Morita emphasizes current circumstances while recognizing that past situations (e.g. the onset of neurotic difficulties) also affect current feelings. Naikan emphasizes the influence of past circumstances on current feelings while recognizing the part played by current situations, as well. In neither case are feelings overemphasized or over-examined beyond their natural role in human existence.

Both Morita and Naikan accent the inadequacy of mere intellectual understanding. Knowing Morita or Naikan theory is insufficient for overcoming neurosis. Understanding theory can be a helpful step in discovering one's own experiential understanding of neurosis and personal growth. However, it is in the experience of doing that one truly discovers the depth of Moritist and Naikan thought and enters the path toward solace. The instructor of Morita and Naikan is merely a guide. The student must make the behavioral effort to discover the benefits of these therapies. Thus, the credit for relief goes to the student, not to the guide.

Neither Morita therapy nor Naikan therapy is a religious pursuit. Each founder independently stated that his method brought successful students to face the roots of religion. Both methods are closer to education than religion. Yet, clearly, each method was strongly influenced by Buddhist psychological thought—Morita by Zen thought, Yoshimoto by Jodo Shinshu thought. Moritist thinking is not exactly the same as Zen thought. Naikanist thinking is not exactly the same as Shinshu thought. But the similarities are undeniable. The approaches of *jiriki* (self-power) Morita and *tariki* (other-power) Naikan are beautifully complementary. They both offer valid perspectives on the human condition. And the well-rounded student benefits from both approaches.

Constructive Living is a Western method of instruction inspired initially by Morita therapy and Naikan. Incorporating Morita and Naikan thought was a natural and fruitful undertaking because of the genuine parallels between the two. Used together, and practiced with innovative applications and techniques developed in the West, Morita and Naikan provide a solid foundation for human development around the world. We appreciate the efforts of our Japanese teachers and colleagues in bringing these methods to our attention. We have extended the ideas and applications of Morita therapy and Naikan therapy beyond their original boundaries. The future will tell us whether these extensions will bear consistently tasty fruit.

TRANSITION

In *Flowing Bridges, Quiet Waters* I wrote of some of the modifications necessary to transform the essence of the Japanese methods of Morita and Yoshimoto into Constructive Living. Here we take a second look at that transformation. Although Constructive Living was inspired by these Japanese methods, quite parallel approaches to human existence may be found in practices within the traditions of Christianity, Judaism, Sufism, Taoism, Zen Buddhism, Tibetan Buddhism, and others. The practices borrowed and modified by Constructive Living are NOT religious, rather they are realistic measures for achieving mental health.

Morita Therapy

The theoretical transition from Morita therapy to Constructive Living involved seeing that the psychological difficulties of *shinkeishitsu* neurotic patients in Japan were similar to the psychological difficulties of Westerners in normal and neurotic moments. Specifically, *shinkeishitsu* patients in Japan try to fix their feelings before completing some task. They are distracted by their efforts to work directly on their fundamentally uncontrollable psychological state. This very attempt to fix feelings before getting on with life appears to underlie much of Western counseling and psychotherapy. We see too many Western clients encouraged to work on their anger, their hidden grief, their self-esteem, their lack of confidence. They are thus inappropriately distracted from the necessary action of daily living. They wait to get their feelings straightened out exactly as the *shinkeishitsu* neurotic does in Japan.

Morita himself wrote that the psychology of *shinkeishitsu* neurosis was also the psychology of "normal" people. Japanese Moritists took this to mean that no special psychological mechanisms need be posited to understand the neurotic disturbance of *shinkeishitsu* patients. In the West we turned the idea around to apply the psychological understanding of *shinkeishitsu* disturbance to "normal" people. We all have "shinky" moments.

Another step involved seeing that the concept of *toraware*, or "obsession," could be applied more broadly to fixations on all sorts of things (e.g. money, status, love, self growth) beyond neurotic symptoms. Again, Morita wrote that everyone has *shinkeishitsu* tendencies, including an inclination toward becoming obsessed to some degree, and that certain circumstances (such as physical illness) magnify these tendencies.

A more radical step involved recognizing that Constructive Living is not psychotherapy at all. Morita called his method re-education. Nevertheless, it remained within the domain of psychiatric medical practice in Japan. My early books about Morita's practice and Yoshimoto's Naikan practice carried the prestigious word "psychotherapy" in the titles. But Constructive Living has moved beyond   sucbnfines. Moreover, Constructive Living looks at suffering and mental functioning in general from a different perspective than that employed by traditional Western psychotherapy or psychological counseling. All feelings are considered to be natural from the Constructive Living perspective—they arise from life circumstances and personal history. Students work on upgrading behavior while the feelings are allowed to run their natural course.

I am not foolish enough to believe that established bastions of psychotherapy in the West or in Japan will readily recognize Constructive Living as a legitimate pursuit and embrace its practice. But there are already a few therapists in the East and in the West who experiment with Constructive Living practice. They incorporate bits and pieces of this educational method in their guidance of others and in their own lives. Their successful results will encourage them to continue and try other Constructive Living approaches. I suspect that elements of Constructive Living will be incorporated into traditional psychotherapeutic approaches over time, and there will come a day when many therapists will believe that they have been practicing in this manner all along. In any case, what is important is relieving the unnecessary suffering in the world. Whether Constructive Living is recognized and credited with its contribution or not is unimportant. Constructive Living can be seen as part of a general trend away from expressive, explorative modalities toward therapeutic styles emphasizing behavioral change and responsibility.

Naikan

The transition from Naikan to Constructive Living involved minor theoretical alterations and a variety of additions to practice. In some respects Naikan was less difficult than Morita to bring to the West, in some ways more difficult.

The founder of Naikan, Ishin Yoshimoto, didn't see his method primarily as a psychotherapy for the neurotic. He believed that anyone who would do Naikan would benefit from it. Thus, there was no need for a broadening of the concept of Naikan application beyond the psychiatric world as there was in Morita. The difficulties came in two forms: One was the aura of religion which accompanies much of Naikan in Japan. The other was the difficulty of intensive Naikan practice.

To be sure, all psychotherapeutic systems and approaches to living more fully in the world have underlying value systems. Naikan's basis was clearly visible to all in Japan. The Naikan method itself grew out of an adaptation of a subsect of Shinshu Buddhist practice. Naikan encountered resistance from those who saw its religious roots and dismissed it on that account. Yoshimoto experienced difficulties presenting Naikan within the prison world after a time because of imagined potential conflicts between church and state. I suspect that most Japanese who know about Naikan see it as an intensive, time-limited practice set apart from everyday life, although the practice may have some effect on daily living afterward. It was important when introducing Naikan practice into the United States to present it as a broader, secular practice and perspective. In Western Europe, in contrast, Naikan is frequently practiced in Buddhist centers and so retains an image associated with religion. In order to allow the American mental health community to give Naikan serious consideration as a therapeutic tool it was necessary to eliminate or reduce the use of words associated with religious practice (salvation, repentance, heaven and hell, and the like) and to demonstrate the solid grounding of Naikan perspectives in everyday life.

The second hurdle was the severity of the week-long intensive practice of Naikan. *Mishirabe*, the original Shinshu practice from which Naikan was derived, involved fasting and going without sleep for long periods. Yoshimoto eased the physical restrictions to a certain degree. Nevertheless, intensive Naikan involves a commitment of time and physical resources. In Japan intensive Naikan is practiced in isolation in special settings for a week or more from 5 A.M. until 9 P.M. each day. A few opportunities for intensive Naikan have been offered in the United States, but those deeply committed Americans who have completed a week of intensive Naikan in the United States or Japan probably numbered less than fifty by 1990. We have introduced Naikan practice in Constructive Living through less demanding assignments and exercises.

Constructive Living assignments include saying "thank you" to a particular person in ten different ways ten times a day, writing letters of thanks and apology to parents and others, doing secret services for others, picking up trash in public places, and so forth. Daily Naikan exercises, shorter periods of Naikan reflection each morning and evening are assigned to some Constructive Living students. In Japan this daily Naikan is usually offered as a sustaining follow-up assignment for those who have completed a week of intensive Naikan. Journal Naikan involves keeping a written record of memories based on the three Naikan themes of what was received from others, what was returned to others, and the troubles caused to others. Journal Naikan is practiced in the West and has been developed greatly in Japan by Ishii Akira.

The utility of Naikan in America is apparent. Our American ethos is supported by psychotherapeutic measures which often aim at discovering the faults of our parents and their contributions to our present problems. However imperfect they may have been, our contributions to their misery, and their positive support of our lives in concrete, detailed ways are frequently ignored. Naikan helps restore a more balanced, realistic perspective. Perhaps Americans believe that in order to achieve independence as adults we must minimize the contributions of others in our childhood and adult lives. Whatever the goal, to disregard reality exacts a price on our daily existence. If we are capable of facing the truth squarely, we benefit from it.

The self-centeredness and greed and meaninglessness in the lives of some Americans is combated by Naikan practice. Appreciation and responsibility and reciprocation increase at the expense of self-deception and selfishness. Notice that the appeal of Naikan isn't described in terms of some religious ideal, but in terms of human values more acceptable to a broader spectrum of the Western public.

LIMITS

What are the limits to the therapeutic benefits of Constructive Living? Who are appropriate and inappropriate students? In Japan Morita therapy was applied to the narrow range of *shinkeishitsu* neurotic patients characterized by perfectionism, idealism, obsessions, compulsions, anxiety disorders, phobias, neurasthenia and similar difficulties. The range of applications is broadening in Japan these days beyond those early limits. Naikan has found application across a wide spectrum of difficulties from sociopathy and neuroses to interpersonal and psychophysical problems.

As evidenced by the chapter in this book contributed by Patricia Ryan Madson, on Constructive Living for the well, it isn't necessary to be suffering in some clinically defined way in order to benefit from the practice of Constructive Living principles. Those who cannot understand the instruction (persons with very low IQ, young children, individuals out of contact with reality because of psychosis or chemicals, and so forth) and people who do not do the experiential exercises for whatever reasons will not find Constructive Living of much use.

Of course, Constructive Living is not a panacea for all human problems. But it is a fundamental resource for many of them. The section on personal experiences with this method will begin to give some idea of the breadth of applications.

Certainly, when illness is involved, medical intervention is appropriate. In the case of schizophrenia, manic depressive disorder, clinical depression or trauma and the like, medical treatment is "something that needs to be done." Constructive Living in no way conflicts with such therapeutic action. On the contrary, Constructive Living provides support for necessary behaviors such as getting to medical appointments, properly taking prescribed medication, dietary restrictions, and healthy daily living.

CURRENTS

Some adaptations were necessary in order to introduce ideas inspired by Morita therapy and Naikan into the West. The essence of the ideas of Morita and Yoshimoto remain within Constructive Living, I believe. Some practitioners of these methods in Japan might disagree. The usefulness of these modifications will become apparent over time. Noteworthy is the trend by which these modifications flow back into Japan and are adopted as standard practice by the Japanese themselves.

In sum, both Morita and Naikan therapies ask the students to look at reality. Morita therapy focuses on current reality, Naikan therapy on past reality. It is the intrusion of unrealistic thinking which is neurosis.

Both Morita and Naikan therapies support the notion of no-self. Morita therapy offers loss of the self in action and in the environment. Naikan therapy offers loss of the self in structured meditation on the past and recognition that all is borrowed. Self-focus or self-centeredness is seen by both to be characteristic of neurosis.

Both Morita and Naikan emphasize experiential understanding. Both see the instructor as an experience guide. Both credit success for cure to the actions of the students. Both are based on Buddhist psychology (Zen and Shinshu Buddhism, respectively), but neither are strictly religious activities.

Constructive Living brings the two Japanese therapeutic systems together in a cohesive whole, then arranges and adopts additional materials from a variety of Japanese and non-Japanese lifeways to provide a broad base for effective human life.

3

THE WATER BOOKS

DAVID K. REYNOLDS

In the Quill Series (published by William Morrow) are a collection of books about Constructive Living. They all have some form of water in the title: *Playing Ball on Running Water, Even in Summer the Ice Doesn't Melt, Water Bears No Scars, Pools of Lodging for the Moon, A Thousand Waves,* and *Thirsty, Swimming in the Lake.* Water is a symbol of flexibility and adaptability. It is essential to our lives. These "water books" have provided more than seventy thousand readers with their first exposure to Constructive Living ideas. The books contain the addresses and telephone numbers of several Constructive Living centers around the United States. Thousands of readers have written and telephoned to thank us or to inquire about methods of further study. In this chapter I offer a miniature version of a water book with new material but similar framework. Thus, the reader will get a taste of the style and content of this less formal body of literature about Constructive Living.

The water books each begin with a brief summary of Constructive Living for those readers who pick up a book in the middle of the series. This introductory material is followed by essays elaborating Constructive Living thought. Then there is material on maxims, the pithy sayings which serve as mnemonic devices to keep Constructive Living principles in mind. Exercises provide a fundamental vehicle for experiential learning within this lifeway. Finally, a substantial section of each book is devoted to what might be called "fairy tales for grownups." These tales provide another channel for accessing the wisdom of this lifeway. The intended meaning of the tales may be elucidated, or the discovery of the tales' meaning may be left to the reader. The format of this chapter follows along the lines of the water books: introduction, essays, maxims, exercises, tales.

INTRODUCTION

Constructive Living is about getting hold of reality. Feeling and ruminating and obsessing are real enough, but when we get lost in such experiences we miss the wider, more varied reality around us. The action aspect of Constructive Living comes from Japan's Morita therapy with its emphasis on attention to surroundings as well as internal events and its suggestion that life is most satisfying when we are engaged in constructive activity. The reflection aspect of Constructive Living comes from Japan's Naikan therapy with its emphasis on recognition of the detailed ways in which our surroundings (including people) have continued to support us even though we weren't paying attention to the support, much less offering thanks.

Constructive Living offers basic, down-to-earth advice about living which can be readily confirmed by everyday experience. Its goals are more in tune with getting along well than getting high on a peak experience. It is easy to understand and hard to practice. But, then, much of what is valuable in life is such.

ESSAYS

Fear of Public Speaking

What kind of advice does Constructive Living offer people who fear speaking in public? An instructor might say something like this:

Your attention is misdirected. You worry about not making a fool of yourself, about how others will receive you. What others think of you isn't controllable directly by your will. Trying to make them like you is a game you can't be sure of winning. What is important is the content of what you say. What is the purpose of your speech? What is the audience? What does your audience need to hear? What do you need to say to them? Self consciousness occurs because one's consciousness is on the self and not on the material for the speech.

You don't need to make special mental efforts to prepare yourself psychologically to speak publicly. You do need to work on polishing the content of your presentation, and perhaps on a smoothly paced delivery. When the material is useful and clear and interesting you become transparent, a vehicle for the display of the substance of your talk.

In case you are required to make a speech with uninteresting material and an uninterested audience you would do well to spend time on spicing up the content and delivery so that you and the audience are naturally drawn into it. Don't waste your time trying to generate confidence in yourself to present material that doesn't deserve confidence. Confidence to do public speaking will come after you have succeeded at it, not before.

Constructive Living on Suffering and Failure

In a recent letter the writer mentioned that she had experienced some pretty difficult times this year and was emerging from them. It is some consolation that difficult times often prompt us to pay close attention to what reality is bringing and to participate in that circumstance fully. We can grow from the experience.

The writer went on to ask, "So why is there suffering in the world? Must I accept all of that suffering as part of reality?" My response:

If I understand your question, you are asking me to pronounce on the necessity of suffering in the world. Such judgment is beyond me. Why reality on the whole is the way it is, I cannot say. But if you ask me whether the suffering in the immediate area surrounding me is necessary I will say that at least some of it is not necessary. Part of my task in the world is to cooperate in the work to reduce that unnecessary suffering which appears before me. When I fail at that task the suffering is increased—at the very least my suffering is added to the total weight of misery because I failed. And even as I work to reduce it I must accept all the suffering which presents itself to me, including my own.

Failure brings me suffering. But failure lies behind much success. In order to give failure the chance to become success it is necessary to continue to take constructive action. Potential success, like any other form of potential, is like collateral: It's only useful when, with help, you can turn it from possibility into reality.

Noticing the Debts

Cars are wonderful devices. I sit on my behind and wiggle my feet with the result that my body is moved great distances. I walked to the post office yesterday, a round trip I usually make in fifteen minutes in the car. It took an hour and a half on foot. Thank you, car.

If one lives in a foreign country for any length of time and must conduct everyday activities in a foreign language, in foreign facilities one learns the importance of ordinary life activities such as laundering, meal preparation, housecleaning, shopping, eliminating, sleeping and so forth. The more difficult they become the more one recognizes their value.

Thanks to this pen I write; not thanks to pens in general. If it weren't for this particular pen then I'd have to make effort to find another specific pen. Reality comes in concrete, specific form—this book, that chair, this moment, that bag. We add the labels/definitions of harmful or beneficial or whatever. The abstractions, generalizations and evaluations are products of our minds, of course. Such an obvious truth should not be forgotten when we engage in neurotic thinking.

Occasions

Weather, guests, and illness. What have these in common? For one thing, they all provide occasions. The circumstances of weather prompt me to get outside while it is sunny and to keep a number of inside activities ready in case of rain. Showing guests the Oregon coast provides me with the opportunity to view those wonders again. Illnesses give me chances to attend to body functions I ordinarily take for granted and to demonstrate nurturance and appreciation to people I too often take for granted.

Occasions are important stimuli in our lives. Reality keeps sending them our way. How we use them molds who we become, is who we are.

MAXIMS

Just knowing is not enough; put knowledge into action.

Reality doesn't reward intent. It can only respond to action.

Adult Children of Alcoholics—People chasing their tales.

The default concern for many is the worry about others' eyes.

Naikan melts the lacquer of life.

Overprotection of a child is *Constrictive Loving*, not Constructive Living.

If you try to preserve something you lose it. If you give something away freely you save it. If you try to keep something the same you kill it. If you allow it to change you keep it alive. If you try to protect something you weaken it. If you encourage it to struggle for itself you strengthen it. Control fosters resistance. Freedom allows appreciation, but doesn't guarantee it.

Constructive Living people make waves, are waves.

EXERCISES

Set goals for the day each morning and review your progress in achieving them each evening. Make sure your goals are specific and concrete and achievable directly by your actions. For example, "being liked by Sally at the office" is unacceptable but "bringing flowers to Sally at the office" is reasonable.

Watch for your strong moments and use them. For example, an invigorating shower might precede that task which requires vigorous activity. After a fine meal you might decide to go shopping for food. A big sale might provide the occasion to talk with your boss about your future in the company.

Paying attention to your surroundings is important, but using that information to inform action is also important. If you notice that the floor needs sweeping then sweep it. If you are in the midst of some other task make a note of what else needs doing so you don't have to carry around a list of activities in your memory.

When one of our Constructive Living instructors puts her hand on the gearshift knob she remembers the person who taught her to drive. When you get ready to drive off think thanks to the person who taught you, the workers who made and serviced your car, the highway maintenance people. Who else contributed to this car trip?

We often use excessive talk to avoid paying attention, to get through time, or to impress and amuse others. Pick at least one day a week to use words thriftily, carefully, purposefully. Notice how easy it is to forget your resolve. When you catch yourself drifting from your purpose return to careful, limited speech.

TALES

Frost

There is frost on the porch railing and the bird feeder and the lawn and roof today. The frost lets us know something about the temperature. Temperature alone won't produce frost, of course. There must be moisture. There must be that water, essential for life, and that circumstance with freezing potential.

Water says, "I won't go away. I'll stick it out."
Cold says, "I'll make it uncomfortable for you."
Water replies, "Yes, you can do that to me."
Cold threatens, "I'll make you change."
Water admits, "Yes, you can do that to me."
Cold says, "Give up!"
But water endures. How beautiful frost makes the world!

Special Powers

As a child Lee was told that certain children had special powers to change the whole course of human history or at least the neighborhood. The powers were variously described to be housed in a box, in a book, in a balloon. Lee was one of those children, Mother said. Certainly Lee was a special child, the teachers confirmed. Lee grew up feeling special. But those special powers were never used. Nevertheless, feeling special altered the course of Lee's childhood and adulthood.

Lifelike People

They were people who danced and drove and made love and ate lunch but they weren't alive. Not really alive. Not all the time. They read and discussed and attended and expressed the "proper" attitudes, but they weren't alive. Not really. At least sometimes. And they worried about whether they were fully alive. At least sometimes.

They wondered what to do to become fully alive. They asked friends and read books and frequented places of enlightened learning. They sought and practiced and meditated and yearned and even grasped. Sometimes.

And they kept changing. Like life.

Star Game

The game is played with these rules: You get points for getting points. You also get points for taking points from others. The fewer points that others have the more points available for you. But if others stop playing the game you must give them points. So you must give others enough points to keep them in the game, but as few as possible.

Those with the most points get to modify the rules of the game to their advantage. Cheating or tampering with the rules by people with too few points is not permitted. But punishing them costs points, an unpleasant prospect.

Giving away points is an important strategy for some players. Accumulating points is the common strategy. Understandably, but lamentably, those with lots of points may be considered to be winners. They could change the game into another one. When does a game become a different one? How does team play fit in this game?

What game are you playing?

Constructive Living need not find application only to the troubled individual with many neurotic moments. It is as useful for the instructor as for the student. The instructor's daily life practice validates and vitalizes the instruction for the student. I am sometimes asked how it is possible to produce so many books. My reply is that, firstly, Constructive Living is about everyday life, so there is an endless supply of material for writing. And, secondly, the discipline of standing in front of a word processor and producing the writing is ordinary life for me, encouraged by Constructive Living principles.
—DKR

4

CONSTRUCTIVE LIVING FOR THE WELL— TOWARD A SUPERIOR LIFE

PATRICIA RYAN MADSON

I am a housewife and a teacher of drama at Stanford University. I have no formal training in psychotherapy, and yet, for the past three years, every day I thought of Morita Shoma and usually mentioned his name. Here I would like to share with the reader some information about Morita's vision of mental health as it is being practiced by a growing number of us in the United States who follow Morita's advice for mental health through the lens of Constructive Living.

For Morita this paradigm was founded on a belief in "natural man" and in his deep desire to live fully (*sei no yokubo*). In the *shinkeishitsu* (shortened to "shink" or "shinky" by Americans) or neurotic individual there is a problem of misplaced attention. By assisting a patient to redirect his attention away from his "symptoms" and toward his purpose through useful work and activity, Morita taught a schema for building

In slightly modified form this chapter was presented as a paper at the First International Congress of Morita Therapy in Hamamatsu, Japan in April, 1990. The paper was subsequently published among the proceedings of the *Journal of Morita Therapy*, volume 1, number 2, 1990.

a superior life. This view teaches the central concept of *"arugamama"* (acceptance of life as it is). For American students the notion that feelings and thoughts are uncontrollable directly by their will, and that they are not responsible for them, is revolutionary and counter to much of mainstream psychotherapy. It is frankly very good news for many who are suffering unnecessarily, and who discover that they don't have to "fix the feelings first." For both the *shinkeishitsu* student and the healthy student this paradigm holds as a model for living a life of meaning.

For the past two years I have been seeing students privately as a Constructive Living teacher. I have seen approximately 50 students who have come for individual instruction, wishing to learn more about applying Morita's principles to their lives. The great majority of these students are in good mental health overall; they come not so much to eliminate a phobia or solve some other problem but to deepen the quality of their lives. "How can I live more fully, more mindfully, with more purpose?" is a common theme.

Using Morita's wisdom, Constructive Living offers sound advice to the person who wants to get more out of life. "Know your purpose." "Accept your feelings." "Do what needs to be done." "Open your eyes and pay attention." "Effort is good fortune."

For many of these students their shinky symptoms arise in the form of excessive worry over life. They "think too much," fantasize and speculate inordinately. This tendency is widespread in the upper middle class population that comes to me, including the majority of Stanford University students whom I teach. Life in the late 1980's and early 1990's in urban San Francisco was, for many people, distant from any sense of nature or the natural rhythms of the seasons. Nature has always been appreciated by the Japanese and well honored in Morita's view. Feelings are natural, Moritist theory holds. The San Francisco earthquake, however, brought nature's hand to our awareness.

Often these students with their answering machines, fax machines, personal computers, cable television with fifty ready channels, and the staggering array of options of merchandise to buy and services and classes to take, find themselves overwhelmed with options and with privileges. They seem to be "thirsty, swimming in the lake". . . to quote a title of one of the CL books (Reynolds, 1991). Indeed, some of these students are nearly "thirsty, drowning in the lake." I have seen that Morita's advice for sensible living crosses cultures very easily and is of particular value and effectiveness for these students.

Constructive Living gently reminds the student that reality itself is the teacher. To start learning all that life has to teach, one has only to begin by paying attention to the details of experience. The central tool of this process is attention. The students need no guru, no textbooks, no mantra, no meditation, no props, and no excuses. They need only to open their eyes, and to look carefully at the world that they are in at that moment. The teacher will coach the students by instructing:

> Please notice everything, and bring your attention back when it wanders. And if you become bored with paying attention, notice that, and continue looking at what's around you. And later if you've become annoyed with yourself for not paying attention well enough, please just look again at the reality of the ordinary world around you.

And once the students are looking at reality the instructor asks them to engage in constructive action, to observe what needs to be done and to do it.

Constructive Living teachers advise the students to begin to notice their personal impact on the reality that they see and experience. The instructors ask them to begin to cultivate that part of themselves which appreciates the miracle of life and notices what comes their way and the ways in which many people and things are constantly serving them. Ultimately Constructive Living invites the students to become part of the solution in this complex world of the 1990's instead of part of the problem.

My students come from a variety of occupations and have various purposes for beginning CL work. They include a doctor who wanted advice on managing his time more effectively, a housewife who was in a deep depression and had given up doing her housework, a therapist seeking advice about finding her purpose in life, a hotel manager who wanted to stop procrastinating and take control of his professional life, a waitress who wanted to improve her daily attention and awareness of life's gifts, a podiatrist who wanted to use the practices of Constructive Living to support and enhance his Zen practice, an urban planner who used Morita's principles in making a major career change, and a graduate student of business with a "Mensa IQ" who was "crippled" by his fear of taking exams. These students reported that they found satisfaction and personal growth through the use of Morita's principles. Included in this volume is a statement by Jim Hutchinson, one of my students, who reports on his experience.

All of these students are in search of a superior life. Each was willing to apply the lessons of Constructive Living to attain that goal. The results have been gratifying. What do I mean by the notion of "superior life"? Is it not arrogant to make such a claim? I think not. A superior life is one in which an individual has faced a fundamental preoccupation with self interest and turned it around. Life energies are turned toward constructive ends and activities. Such a person sees himself or herself as part of a larger picture of humanity, as part of a family, a community, a society and the world. This individual looks beyond the self, noticing what reality brings, noticing what needs to be done in every situation and doing it. This person may be counted on to act, to perform, to contribute.

The individual who practices this lifeway may come to experience ordinary life as dense, rich, varied, precious and intrinsically interesting. Once this door has opened, as one student put it: "There is no time out and no turning back." A superior life, indeed.

Constructive Living instructors have their own styles of presenting the content of this lifeway. It is one of the strengths of Constructive Living that an instructor need not use the words of Morita or Yoshimoto or Reynolds or some other teacher to present these ideas. In the following chapter Rami Shapiro guides us through some introductory concepts, noting along the way various doubts and challenges which arise in the minds of the students. Thanks to the questions and comments of our students we are able to refine our presentations in such a way as to make them more comprehensible. —DKR

5

CONSTRUCTIVE LIVING,
A FIRST LOOK

RAMI M. SHAPIRO

INTRODUCTION

Over the past few years I have been running a series of one-day seminars entitled "Introduction to Constructive Living." Each seminar is structured around four questions:

What Do I Want Out Of Life?
How Do I Go About Getting What I Want Out of Life?
Does This Work?
What Else Can I Do?

A general outline of the seminar looks like this:

9:00 A.M.–10:30 A.M. Question One
10:30 A.M.–10:50 A.M. Break
10:50 A.M.–12:00 P.M. Question Two
12:00 P.M.–12:45 P.M. Lunch
12:45 P.M.–2:15 P.M. Question Three
2:15 P.M.–2:30 P.M. Break
2:30 P.M.–3:30 P.M. Question Four
3:30 P.M.–4:00 P.M. Conclusion

What follows is a summary of the content and process of these seminars.

WHAT DO I WANT OUT OF LIFE?

After the normal introductory and logistic matters are dealt with, I divide the participants into smaller groups of ten people or fewer. Each group selects a secretary who is given a flip chart and thick-tipped marker with which to record the group's responses to the question, What do I want out of life? While I do not insist upon a specific brainstorming method, I do suggest that each person in the group be asked for a single response, going around as many times as necessary until each person signifies that he or she has no further responses to offer. The exercise takes approximately one half hour. At the end of the period I ask that the flip chart sheets be taped to the walls so that each group can read the others' responses.

It is not surprising to find that groups list similar items. I ask that each group present its list, reading and, if necessary, elaborating upon each item. As a group's list is read it is the job of the other secretaries to cross off similar items from their own lists so that each group presents only new items. The readings take about fifteen minutes and result in a master list of what the entire group wants out of life.

I then ask the groups to consider the kinds of issues contained in the list and to mark each item as belonging to one of two categories: Controllable (C) and Uncontrollable (U). During this time I create a two-column master list based on my own assessment of each item. Samples from a typical list look like this:

WHAT DO I WANT OUT OF LIFE?

CONTROLLABLE	UNCONTROLLABLE
behavior	happiness
	grandchildren
	peace of mind
	success
	love
	security
	health

I present my two-column master list as a working text and begin a serious exploration of the notion of controllable and uncontrollable. For many if not most of the participants the notion that certain very intimate parts of their lives are not under the direct control of their will is a new idea. The following conversation is typical of the kind of dialogue the master list engenders:

> Young Woman (YW): Why place "happiness" in the Uncontrollable column? I put it under Controllable; I can control happiness.
>
> RMS: The list reflects my own experience and may not fit everyone. What about the rest of you—can you control happiness? (Murmur of mixed responses.)
>
> Older Man (OM): I don't think so. Happiness is dependent on other people, other variables beyond my control.
>
> YW: Yes, but you can control your responses to those other things. I know I can't control you, but I can control how I feel about you.
>
> RMS: You have raised a key issue; Can you control how you feel?
>
> YW: Of course. My feelings, my thoughts, my brain.. . .
>
> Older Woman (OW): I'm not so sure. I mean it is my brain but sometimes I find myself thinking thoughts I don't want to think or feeling things. . . sometimes my feelings catch me by surprise.
>
> RMS: Suggesting a lack of control?
>
> YW to OW: But once you are aware of them can you turn them off?
>
> OW: I try. I tell myself not to think this or that. But the more I do that the more I end up thinking about it.
>
> RMS to YW: Let's try an experiment. For the next thirty seconds stop thinking about this seminar. Start now, we'll wait. (Laughter.)
>
> YW: Well, I can't do that. I mean I'm sitting here. I'd have to leave and do something else. You know, distract myself.
>
> RMS: Yes! Now you have it. When we do something else the something else generates new thoughts that crowd out the old thoughts at least for a time. This we can do. But without

action, without changing our behavior and engaging in some other activity, can we by some effort of will change our way of thinking? Can we will ourselves to feel angry or happy or sad, or do thoughts and feelings simply pop into our minds of their own accord?

The dialogue continues for quite some time taking up other items on our list as examples. The point is very simple: control is a useful term only with regards to behavior. Thoughts, feelings and attitudes are not perfectly controllable by the will, though we seem to have more control over what we think than over what we feel. While not every participant agrees with this assessment, even those in opposition will play along as if this were so in order to benefit from the rest of the seminar. A twenty-minute break follows this discussion.

HOW DO I GET IT?

Returning to the Master List we now take up the question, How do I go about securing the things I want out of life? Depending upon the item, the responses vary; yet it is not hard to discover a trend. The item in the Controllable column is the only aspect of our lives that is directly controllable. Items under the Uncontrollable column are pursued by behavioral effort and by accepting or indirectly influencing feelings.

An example that some might mistakenly put in the Controllable column is "health." If I am pursuing good health I must control my diet, initiate and maintain a regular exercise program, follow a regime of good hygiene, establish a daily period of meditation or relaxation, and so forth. All of these behaviors are controllable. I may choose to do them or not to do them, but there is no question that if I choose the former I increase the likelihood of accomplishing my goal. Strictly speaking, the result of good health isn't guaranteed even if we do all the "right" things. While such behavior cannot guarantee good health, it does promote it. The absence of such behavior, while not precluding good health, will maximize the likelihood of ill health.

An example from the Uncontrollable column is "peace of mind." A typical reaction to placing peace of mind in the Uncontrollable category is the following argument put forth by a graduate (G) of several mind control seminars:

G: Wait a minute. My peace of mind is totally under my control. I am only a thought away from happiness at any moment.

RMS: Yes, that is so. At any moment we are a thought away from any other thought. The question is whether or not we are capable of controlling that missing thought. Right now, for example, you are agitated by the thought that I am presenting a falsehood to the group. You are anxious to present the truth and protect your opinion. You may even feel anger towards me for placing you in the position of having to correct me. At this moment where is your peace of mind?

G: Yeah, I don't know, but it is there. . . just beneath the surface.

RMS: Are you at peace now? Your voice suggests you are not.

G: No, not at the moment but. . .

RMS: Can you please demonstrate your position by thinking the thought that will bring you peace of mind?

G: Now?

RMS: Please.

G: Well, it doesn't work that way. I'm too upset. I'd have to get up and walk outside or something. Get away, clear my head.

RMS: Peace of mind cannot be conjured by thought?

G: Not like by just thinking, no.

RMS: Your thoughts of peace are not directly controllable by will?

G: If you mean can I just think myself cool, forget it.

RMS: Then we are in agreement. We cannot think ourselves cool; we cannot think ourselves anything. Feelings and thoughts arise of their own accord and are not directly controllable by our will. Any attempt to feel ourselves or wish ourselves or think ourselves into achieving the goals we have set for ourselves will, unless accompanied by action, be doomed to failure.

Man: Doesn't positive thinking have any effect?

RMS: All I'm saying is that if we wait for positive thoughts and feelings to generate the actions that will work toward securing our goals we may well wait forever. If I do what must be done only when I feel like it, I may never get started and I certainly won't finish. Feelings are too fluid to be the basis of action.

Discussion as to how we go about achieving our life's goals continues until lunch. The purpose of the discussion is to help the participants grasp the essential difference between feeling-centered and action-centered approaches to life. I suggest we continue exploring these ideas informally over lunch. After lunch and clean up we return to our seats and take up Question Three: Does It Work?

DOES IT WORK?

With question three we begin to explore how successful our feeling-based approach to life is with regard to achieving our life goals. It is easy to see that, for the items in our Controllable column, hard work and perseverance increase our chances of success. At the very least we can agree that lack of behavioral effort will often insure failure. But what about those items listed in the Uncontrollable column? Here is a portion of a much longer conversation about love:

Man in Mid-Forties (M): Our talk of love seems awfully cold. It sounds like we are saying that love is just manipulation. I only act lovingly in order to get my lover to love me. I'm not manipulating when I bring my wife flowers. I just bring them.

RMS: With no ulterior motive? No desire other than to please? No thoughts of "If she is happy she will . . ."

M: Well, if she is in a good mood she certainly is easier to get along with. . . .

RMS: But you don't buy her flowers to precipitate the mood. . . .

M: Well, not consciously, but I guess. . . now that I'm thinking. . . It doesn't sound right, but I guess that is true in my mind somewhere.

RMS: Please don't get me wrong, I'm not opposed to buying flowers. Nor do I wish to make your experience fit some preset idea. All I'm asking is that you look honestly at what is happening and see if sometimes what we call love is not at least tinged by our desires to influence another to our own ends. When we have that goal, to influence another, we can't be sure that our actions will produce the effect we want. As a matter of fact, we can never be sure our actions will produce the effect we want.

If you bring home flowers because you know that this is a loving thing to do whether or not you are feeling particularly loving at the moment of purchase, then you are simply doing what needs doing. You aren't depending on whether some uncontrollable goal is being achieved or not. Even if you come home and find your wife in a sour mood you still know that you have acted constructively. But if you are buying the flowers specifically to change her mood, you may be disappointed. Or if you wait to feel in the mood yourself, you may never buy another bouquet again. If the deed is right, then the doing takes precedence over the feeling and over the desired result.

M: And what if the mood and the doing coincide?

RMS: Wonderful! Just don't wait for that to happen before you act. You'll enjoy it when it happens, but don't base your life on it.

Woman nursing a child: I guess you could say that about most things. I'm feeding my baby to ward off the guilt I would experience if she starved to death. But does that really get at the totality of my action? Does it help me to be a better person? I mean if I only nursed when I felt like it rather than when she needed it, she would go hungry.

RMS: Exactly. Good analogy. You do what must be done— in this case feeding. What is your daughter's name? Feeding Melissa because she needs to be fed whether or not you feel like it. We must do loving things whether or not we feel love at the moment or not. What do we know about feelings?

Group: They are uncontrollable.

RMS: Right. Sometimes I feel loving, sometimes not. But if I want love, if I want someone to treat me in a loving way, I increase the likelihood of that by doing loving things for that person. Anyway, the doing of the loving deeds changes me.

Man: There is still manipulation here. You are doing something to get something back in return. What's the difference?

RMS: I have not said anything about getting rid of the desire for love. Desires are feelings, and feelings are uncontrollable, so there is no talk about getting rid of desire. I want to be loved. I suspect you do too. Sometimes I feel love toward someone else, sometimes not. But if I wait to feel love in order to do loving deeds my life is unnecessarily restricted. Unconditional love may be possible, but this takes us beyond the scope of our discussion. Staying with the everyday conditionality of things, can we act in loving ways even when we don't feel like it?

Man: Sure, but it is hypocrisy. Honesty demands that I act from my feelings. That I say what I think.

Woman: He's right! God, I tell my husband over and over again: "Tell me what you're feeling for God's sake!" The man is hard as a rock (laughter). . .Oh. No pun intended. . .(more laughter)

RMS: Honesty demands that we be honest. And when we are honest with our feelings what do we find? Look into it now and see how feelings operate. Are they steady, constant, or are they complex and changing from moment to moment?

Woman: No, they change. Even when I'm mad or something I can sense other feelings mixed in. Hurt, jealousy, or something.

RMS: So from which of these shifting feelings do we respond? Which of them is the honest feeling that will save us from hypocrisy?

Man: You can't do that—separate them out. They are all real, just flowing so fast that you can't pull them apart.

RMS: Feelings come and go. If we acted on each and every thought and feeling we experienced during a given day, what would happen?

Woman: Chaos.

Man: They'd have to put me away. In jail or a sanitarium. God, if I acted on every thought and feeling I'd never accomplish anything worthwhile. . . .

Woman: So what are you saying? We should ignore feelings? Isn't that the problem—we ignore our feelings?

RMS: I don't know if that's the problem, but I can tell you it isn't my problem. I don't know how to ignore my feelings. Feelings are for feeling, and I can't help but feel them. I wouldn't want to be without my feelings. They are valuable sources of information which I ignore at my peril. All I'm suggesting is that while feelings are for feeling they may not be the best foundation upon which to base my behavior.

Man: Sounds like you want to be a Vulcan like Star Trek's Spock.

RMS: No. Vulcans have erased their capacity to feel. I value feelings as tremendously important sources of information. I want to feel and feel deeply. But I am afraid to do that if I let those feelings dictate my behavior. If I take control of my behavior I free myself to feel whatever feelings arise. I can feel as sexy, as angry, as despicable as possible and yet not act sexy, angrily or despicably.

Eventually the conversation clarifies the following points:

1. Some of our interactions with others may be aimed at influencing them to behave in ways that will generate specific feelings in ourselves.

2. When desired feelings arise we may mistakenly try to hold on to them by our will.

3. When undesired feelings arise we may mistakenly seek to will them away.

4. When these undesired feelings persist or when the desired feelings fail to arise on command we may blame the other person for failing to properly respond to our will.

5. We may believe that this failure on their part generates anger in us which, we may believe, causes a heated exchange of accusations—"If you really loved me you would . . ."

While not everyone will see things this way (and getting agreement on these points is never my aim) still most will recognize some truth in what is offered. To the extent that they identify with this assessment they are interested in finding out what they can do to avoid feeling-centered interpersonal difficulties in the future. Even people who rarely fall into manipulative feeling-based behavior are likely to want to learn how to prevent or reduce such incidents even further. A fifteen-minute break follows our discussion, after which we move on to question four: What Else Can I Do?

WHAT ELSE CAN I DO?

Constructive Living is a powerful response to this question, and it is only with the introduction of this final question that I begin to formally use the term Constructive Living. The presentation sounds something like this:

If feeling-based responses to life are not effective, what else can we employ? Let me suggest three principles to guide your actions from this day forward. These principles are based on the work of Dr. Shoma Morita (1874–1938), a Japanese psychiatrist, physician and department chairman at Jikei University School of Medicine in Tokyo. Dr. Morita believed that much of our suffering is rooted in a basic misunderstanding of life. We need to discover anew how life operates. In fact that is what we have been doing throughout this seminar.

Exploring these experienced facts of life we discovered that our life goals fall into two categories: controllable and uncontrollable. We learned that feelings and thoughts are, relative to behavior, uncontrollable. Uncontrollable, of course, is not the same as undesirable. Sometimes pleasant, sometimes not, these fluctuations of mind are sources of important information that I must access if I am to make coherent life choices. We also learned that the controllable elements in our lives are behavioral, that no matter how I feel I can choose how I will act. We learned that a feeling-based response to life is not necessarily the most fruitful, rational, or appropriate way of achieving our goals. We learned that much of our lives is taken up in pursuit of or escape from feelings and thoughts over which we have little or no direct control.

From what we ourselves have discovered we might be able to formulate Dr. Morita's principles inductively on our own. Yet in the interest of continuity with the language of Constructive Living let me give you the standard formulation of the three major Moritist principles:

Know Your Purpose;
Accept Your Feelings;
Do What Must Be Done.

Know your purpose. What do you want out of life? This is the question with which we opened our discussion. Our goals can be grand or simple, distant or immediate, but, without keeping them in mind, we will never achieve them. The clearer we are as to what we want, the clearer we are as to how to appropriately (ethically, morally, etc.) go about achieving it.

Accept your feelings. How do we usually go about achieving our purpose? Through feeling-based effort. We seek to feel right before we act rightly. Accepting my feelings means that, as I open myself to the wealth of information flooding my mind moment to moment, I discover that not all of that information is useful or appropriate. No use fighting feelings, all we need do is accept them, learn from them, and act rightly regardless of how they play themselves out.

Do what must be done. At each moment we are presented with things to do, many of which we do not feel like doing. Accept these feelings, recall your purpose, and do those things that are necessary to achieve that purpose. You want to do well in school but you don't feel like studying? Accept that and study anyway. You're dieting and you have a tremendous desire to eat that slice of chocolate cake. Accept the desire and don't eat the cake.

It sounds so simple, but do not mistake "simple" for "easy." Constructive Living is not easy. It requires attention, discipline and a willingness to openly acknowledge what is happening within and around us.

Will Constructive Living guarantee happiness? No, happiness is a feeling and feelings rise and fall of their own accord. We influence them indirectly through behavior but we can never control them. Mentioning our lack of control over feelings sometimes prompts a discussion of the sense of trying anything at all:

Man: So why bother?

RMS: Results and behavior are not always in perfect harmony. There may be other factors which impact on the success of our endeavors. I may work hard to get a certain job and find that for reasons beyond my control the job was offered to someone else. Right action does not guarantee success. But inappropriate action often guarantees failure.

Success or failure are not ours to control, though we can influence them. We influence them through right action; wishing it so is not enough, we must do. And, it is safe to say, if we do wisely we will sometimes succeed. As Dr. Morita put it: "Effort is good fortune." The doing itself becomes its own reward. This is the secret to Constructive Living. When we begin to discover that action, not feelings, is the key to living well, we begin to find pleasure in doing even the simplest of things.

Man: But isn't pleasure a feeling?

RMS: Of course. Constructive Living is not opposed to feelings. On the contrary, it frees us to feel. If I know that my feelings will not dictate my behavior I am free to feel things that hitherto I would try, albeit unsuccessfully, to suppress. Paraphrasing Jay Leno's Dorito's commercial: "Feel all you want, we'll make more." There is no end to feeling. We must simply learn to accept our emotions and go about the business at hand.

Older Woman (OW): But what if I am feeling guilty about an act I am about to commit. A bad act. Should I just ignore the feeling and do it anyway, like, "Who cares?"

RMS: Feelings cannot be ignored. Feelings provide us with important information. If I am feeling guilty it is vital that I examine the proposed action to see if it fits my ideals of rightness, fairness, justice, etc.

OW: But what if the person is a sociopath?

RMS: Some theories hold that such a person feels nothing, and that would be dangerous, if true. We want to feel, we want to take our feelings seriously, but we do not want to base our behavior on them.

The point isn't to feel or not to feel, but how to deal with our feelings. We cannot control feelings directly by our will. Rather, it is through action that we influence thoughts and feelings. When I do something well, I sense a feeling of joy and accomplishment. My responsibility is to the doing; let the feeling arise of its own accord.

Woman: What about feelings that are there and you can't get rid of them? Like depression.

RMS: Can you will yourself out of a depression? If we could simply think ourselves happy wouldn't we be happy all the time? It isn't that simple. We cannot will ourselves to feel, we can only act in constructive ways and allow the feelings to rise and fall of their own accord. So I am depressed. Does it help to yell at myself to get "undepressed"? No. What helps? Doing. Moving the body. Taking a walk. Washing the dog. Cleaning the house. Doing the dishes. Exercising.

Woman: These will distract me from my pain, not get rid of it.

RMS: When you are distracted, that is to say when you are no longer feeling depressed, are you depressed? If a feeling is not being felt is it a feeling for you?

True, your actions may at first be distractions. That's fine. Your purpose in moments of depression may be to become undepressed, and physical effort may help accomplish that so you distract yourself. The house gets cleaned. But later, as your application and mastery of the Constructive Living lifeway deepens, you will do because the doing needs to be done: You wash the dog because the dog is dirty, You exercise because exercise is healthy for you, You do what is right even when you don't feel like it. And the result of this effort? "Effort is good fortune!" The effort may well break the cycle of negative feelings and generate new, perhaps more positive feelings. But that is not the real goal. Effort itself is the goal of Constructive Living. And the dog gets clean.

Man: But if she is depressed because of the death of a loved one, washing the dog won't help.

Second Woman: Or if she is hurting from a bad relationship.

RMS: True. We are talking about first steps. Let's return to our principles. Know your purpose. Her purpose is to live constructively in spite of grief. Accept your feelings. Grief is natural and appropriate. She should not try to avoid the grief, but learn to carry it with her as she slowly returns to a more active life. If she engages life purposefully, time will ease the pain. She may make the unhealthy choice to do things which will sustain her feelings of grief longer than is necessary.

Similarly, if I am in a bad relationship, doing the dishes is not going to change that relationship. Until I do something about the relationship, I am doomed to experience these negative feelings time and again. Again let's recall our three Constructive Living principles. What is my purpose? To enter into a healthy relationship. My feelings tell me that I am locked into a negative relationship. Accept that; it is important information. And then do what must be done. Get the abused woman to a battered woman's shelter, if that is appropriate. Talk to her partner, if that is right. Insist on getting professional help, and then go out and get it. Act. Only by doing will things change. Wishing things would change without working to effect change does nothing to alter the status quo.

Questions like these continue for the final hour. There is no attempt to present or convince. My goal is simply to provide an opportunity for dialogue. My obligation is simply to be as clear with my words as possible and to facilitate clarity of thought in others. I have found Constructive Living to be a great boon to my life, and it is that experience that I wish to share. Doing that to the best of my ability, I trust the truth of what I have experienced to resonate in others and show them the way as well. My experience thus far has shown this approach to be a great success.

CONSTRUCTIVE LIVING
AND SOCIETY

Beginning at the beginning. How early can a child incorporate these life principles? What needs to be taught a child, and what is the best way to teach? How can Constructive Living be used in the remedial nurturance of a disturbed child? Mary J. Puckett moves our thinking along the lines of these issues. Furthermore, she offers some thoughtful initial answers to the questions she raises.   —DKR

6

CONSTRUCTIVE LIVING AND MORITA THERAPY: SOME POSSIBLE APPLICATIONS TO CHILD REARING

MARY J. PUCKETT

INTRODUCTION

Constructive Living has implications for child rearing that have received little previous attention. Although some ideas of Constructive Living are inconsistent with traditional Western approaches to child rearing, many of the principles regarding purpose and feelings would be a useful adjunct to, or replacement for, some traditional ideas. Some basic ideas from the Constructive Living literature are presented with possible applications to child rearing. Parents involved in Constructive Living might teach the principles and practice to their children through both modeling and direct instruction.

Morita therapy originated primarily as a specialized treatment for *shinkeishitsu* adult clients. Like most psychotherapies, it has been found most effective with those who are "average

The assistance of Diana Peterson in reviewing a draft of this article is gratefully acknowledged.

or above-average in intelligence, non-sociopathic, self-reflective, psychologically minded, and motivated to overcome their problems" (Ishiyama, 1988, p. 60). Naikan therapy is suitable for a somewhat wider range of clients, and is based on the principle that a perspective of gratitude has a salutary effect on some common psychological complaints (Reynolds, 1983). Morita and Naikan principles have been combined (Reynolds, 1984a, 1984b, 1986, 1987) and presented, along with some ideas which Reynolds believes make the principles more useful to Westerners, as Constructive Living.

MORITA THERAPY AND CONSTRUCTIVE LIVING

Constructive Living attempts to be broader in both theory and practice than traditional clinical Morita therapy (Reynolds, 1986). It incorporates the principles of Morita therapy (Reynolds, 1984b) as well as the basic concepts of Naikan (Reynolds, 1986). Reynolds increasingly includes ideas from a variety of other sources as part of Constructive Living (e.g., Reynolds, 1989).

Constructive Living is like Morita in being educational in nature, but is intended to address the needs of a broader range of individuals. Reynolds asserts that "Morita's ideas are practical and useful to everyone, not just to *shinkeishitsu* neurotics" (Reynolds, 1986, p. 109). The practice of Constructive Living includes techniques drawn from a variety of sources, including Morita therapy. A major difference is that Morita therapists traditionally have been mental health professionals or physicians, but Constructive Living guides need not be mental health professionals and often are not.

CHILD REARING: WESTERN APPROACHES

At present, the most common approaches to child rearing in the West could be broadly classified as behavioral or developmental in orientation. The behavioral approach (e.g., Dinkmeyer & McKay, 1983; Krumboltz & Krumboltz, 1972; Patterson, 1976) involves obtaining appropriate behavior through controlling consequences to the child. The approach is very effective, and very much in keeping with the twentieth-century Western notion that existence is governed by cause and effect relationships, all of which are subject to rational explanation and ultimately subject to control.

The developmental approach (e.g., Dobson, 1987; Ginsburg & Opper, 1969; Ilg & Ames, 1955) is based on predictable stages of development observed in most children as they grow. This approach, too, can be effective in socializing children. Appropriate behavior is obtained in part by dealing with children in terms of their "needs," which are inferred from behavior and current developmental level.

Both of these approaches are adaptable to the personal values of the parents, and either one is effective for most children. The choice depends more on chance or the background of the parents than on the demonstrated superiority of either system. Either approach would be compatible with Constructive Living, which might be used to provide an enriched philosophical framework to help the child avoid strict determinism or self-centered choices and, in the end, choose "what needs doing."

CONSTRUCTIVE LIVING IDEAS

Marital relationships have not received much attention as such in traditional Morita therapy, but have been considered to some extent in Constructive Living (Reynolds, 1986). In addition, the principles underlying both Morita therapy and Constructive Living, with their emphasis on facing life "as it is," have implications for child rearing. A primary goal in raising children is to provide them with a view of reality and their place in it that will enable them to behave properly. A primary goal of Constructive Living is to learn to clearly perceive reality (including purpose, feelings, and whatever else is present in the current situation) in order to do what needs doing. The overarching purpose of Constructive Living, then, is essentially to help adults become more mature individuals in much the way that responsible adults try to socialize children into adulthood.

CONSTRUCTIVE CHILD REARING

Attention to Effort

Mindfulness, or full attention to any endeavor, is a central part of Constructive Living and is taken directly from Morita therapy (Reynolds, 1976). The effort with which a task is performed, rather than the outcome of the effort, is what is evaluated (Reynolds, 1984a). The effort brought to a task is all that can be controlled by an individual, and good effort is sufficient regardless of the outcome.

A frequently heard complaint about contemporary child rearing is that parents push their children too hard for high achievement academically, socially, or athletically. This problem and the resulting stress might be avoided if parents focused on effort rather than outcome in guiding their children's behavior.

Children learn by practicing things many times, but they must first learn that practice is necessary and rewarding. Children print the alphabet many times before the letters are correctly formed. If they are encouraged in their best efforts, without undue emphasis on perfect outcomes, they learn to value their efforts and gain self-esteem. Success is measured in terms of the child's own efforts, rather than the product of that effort.

This approach may prove useful in later life, when one's efforts on any project (for example, a research proposal) may be good work, but may not be successful (funded), as judged by others, for a variety of reasons outside the control of the individual (e.g., lack of funds, low priority compared to other projects).

Shinkeishitsu Symptoms

The shinkeishitsu symptoms for which Morita therapy is effective with adults also are present in children. There is already a considerable literature about the treatment of anxieties, phobias, and stress in children and adolescents (e.g., Carlson, Figueroa, & Lahey, 1986). Parents utilizing the principles of Constructive Living in their own lives would have strategies to deal with these problems. One valuable lesson children could learn from parents who use the principles of Constructive Living is that fears are acceptable as feelings but need not determine behavior.

To offer a clinical example, we recently had a child in our upstairs office and needed to return him to his mother in the main floor waiting room. At the time the stairs were inconveniently obstructed by furniture being relocated. Although I am afraid of heights, I redirected the child to the fire escape and began to lead him down that way. The child stopped at the door, clinging to the door frame, and said, "I think I'll just wait for the furniture to move." He had learned, probably from his parents and from other representatives of the general culture, to allow fear to control his behavior.

Acceptance of Feelings

"Feelings must be recognized and accepted as they are" (Reynolds, 1984a, p. 10) and "Every feeling, however unpleasant, has its uses" (Reynolds, 1984a, p. 11) are ideas from Morita therapy (Fujita, 1986) that have been incorporated into Constructive Living. The psychodynamic theory of emotions as forces within the individual is so widely accepted that most parents who are aware of feelings believe their children have to "get their feelings out." At the other extreme, we frequently encounter parents who are unable to recognize or accept any feelings from a child: "You aren't really hungry; you ate an hour ago," or "You don't really mind losing that ball; it was old anyway."

A more effective approach to feelings might be used by a parent practicing Constructive Living. Adults using CL in their own lives recognize and accept their own feelings, making it possible to do the same for the feelings of others. They recognize that feelings are not directly controllable and therefore not necessarily subject to logic. Feelings simply arise on their own and exist in their own right: the feeling of hunger has no need to relate logically to having eaten an hour ago; the feeling of sadness at losing a ball need not relate to the age of the ball or to having a dozen other balls as replacements.

The practitioner of Constructive Living knows, practices, and teaches children that acceptance of feelings does not necessarily mean that feelings lead directly to behavior. Other aspects of reality also must be considered in deciding on a course of action. If we accept that the child is hungry (even if the last meal was an hour ago), we still need to consider several other factors before providing a snack. In seeing us review these factors, the child learns that there are other considerations. When is the next scheduled meal? Are we in a setting where eating is appropriate? Is acceptable food available now or do we need to wait? Far too many parents fear they must give in behaviorally if they accept a child's feelings. In fact, the feelings deserve acceptance just as they are, but the decision about behavior depends on purpose and other aspects of reality as well as feelings.

Feelings Fade

"Feelings fade in time unless they are restimulated" (Reynolds, 1984a, p. 11), or, "Emotion will gradually fade away in a parabola if it is left alone, as it is, to run its course naturally" (Fujita, 1986, p. 61). Preschool children have trouble waiting in line or tolerating discomfort because they lack the perspective that all things, including the feeling in the present moment, come to an end. Many adults similarly lack the perspective that feelings will naturally change over time. The popular idea that feelings must be gotten out somehow to avoid psychological problems leads well-meaning parents to try to help children "work through" or get rid of their feelings about life's difficulties rather than accepting the feelings and allowing emotions to change over time. For example, a parent may encourage a child to discuss at length his feelings about a divorce, thus continuously restimulating the child's unhappy feelings rather than allowing the child to turn his attention to a task that needs doing in the present.

An approach more likely to be adopted by a parent involved with Constructive Living would be to teach appropriate expression of feelings and then acknowledge them, while modeling attention to what needs doing in the present as well as to feelings. The child would be encouraged to recognize feelings and express them appropriately. The focus would be on reality in terms of the needs of the moment and purpose rather than on the "If only" and "I wish" that are a part of a child's thinking about divorce. If a child is treated this way, most questions about an issue such as divorce will deal with matters of practical significance, often in the present. If these concerns are addressed as they arise, rather than denied or overemphasized, the child will be more likely to go on with his or her life and allow the parents to get on with theirs rather than trying to punish the parents for divorcing or trick them into reuniting.

Behavior Influences Feelings

"Feelings can be indirectly influenced by behavior" (Reynolds, 1984a, p. 12). Many people mistakenly believe that behavior must await motivation, that they have to "feel like" doing something in order to do it. Consequently, they are susceptible to boredom when there is nothing they "feel like" doing. "I'm bored" is a frequent complaint from children. A parent practicing Constructive Living should be at an advantage in dealing with such complaints. The most effective cure for boredom is to do something—almost anything except sit around complaining of boredom. A Constructive Living parent will have modeled for children the practicality that one can get busy doing something whether one feels like it or not, and will encourage children to do so. A list of possible activities on the refrigerator might provide a starting place, and bored children might change the boredom simply by changing their behavior: pick an activity from the list and begin.

Responsibility for Behavior

"We are responsible for what we do no matter how we feel at the time" (Reynolds, 1984a, p. 14). This is a very important part of the Constructive Living message for parents. Parents have moments when they are not at their best, when they become irritable or unreasonable with a child. In such instances, even an otherwise responsible adult sometimes resorts to the excuse, "I couldn't help it." One mother told us, "When I saw he'd written his initials on the car seat, I just started screaming at him." In reality, if this mother will honestly review her behavior, she will likely notice that she does not lose her temper nearly so easily with her boss, her husband, or others who are likely to retaliate effectively.

Constructive Living suggests a high standard of parenting, and of behavior in general. It asserts that we never truly "lose" control, but are in fact responsible for our behavior. While feelings offer important information about behavior, they are not the only force that drives behavior. Duty, purpose, and other realities of the situation are additional sources of important information in making decisions about action. Parents practicing Constructive Living would hold themselves to these principles, thus requiring that they nurture a child by behaving in a responsible, positive way even when upset. In doing so, such parents also would model responsible behavior. Children would thus learn that they, too, are responsible for their behavior regardless of their feelings.

If more parents would adopt this practice, we might see fewer "out of control" teens in our offices. While parents might at first find it frustrating not to yell at their children, there should be fewer frustrated parents in the long run.

COGNITIVE BEHAVIOR MODIFICATION

Children naturally talk to themselves, and the cognitions which are covert in most adults are thus readily observable in children. Morita therapy has been called a kind of cognitive behavior therapy (Ishiyama, 1986), but the self-talk used in Morita therapy or Constructive Living is significantly different from that used in most forms of cognitive behavior modification.

Common applications of cognitive behavior therapy with children include stress management (Cautela & Groden, 1978; Sanders & Turner, 1983) and impulse control (Camp & Bash, 1981). The cognitive behavior therapy approach to stress management is often through relaxation or reframing. For example, children experiencing stress related to the demands of a highly structured school might be taught to take a few minutes to breathe deeply and relax between classes, and to simultaneously imagine walking in a quiet forest. They also might be instructed to reframe the situation by practicing affirmations of behavioral intentions, such as, "I know how to manage this situation. I can remember what I need to take to class."

A Morita therapy or Constructive Living approach to stress management might begin with the idea of living in this moment and attending fully, even if worried, anxious, or otherwise under stress. Therefore, the same children might deal with stress in school by focusing on the present and what needs doing now. Rather than relaxing and imagining being in a forest, they might be instructed to attend to the business that must be taken care of between classes, such as getting to the locker, sorting through books and materials to prepare for the next class, and getting to class in the most efficient manner possible. Rather than affirming the ability to handle the situation, they would simply handle it. With Constructive Living's addition of Naikan, children also might be instructed to practice covert self-talk about the ways in which support is provided by the school, books, and teachers, rather than exclusive concern with the stress caused by them.

This suggestion may seem rather unlikely in view of the behavior of many adolescents seen in therapy. However, we observe often in therapy that the child or adolescent's coping strategies are very much like those of the parents. The child who is stressed by school may come from a home where the parents are stressed by their attempts to control too many life variables. Parents who focus on what needs doing now and whose self-talk and conversation are about appreciation, rather than stress, probably influence their children to cope in similar ways.

In addition to different covert (cognitive) behavior, children reared by parents involved with Constructive Living may demonstrate overt behavior different from their peers' in several ways. While "know your purpose" is no antidote for the identity crisis of adolescence, knowing a moment-to-moment purpose should be very helpful in getting through adolescence one day at a time, as it has to be lived. Adolescence is the time for developing career plans and other longer-term purposes, as well.

One of the primary problems faced by the adolescents we see is that they do have purposes, but are easily distracted from them by the emotions of the moment. Adolescents who have been trained from childhood to identify purpose, accept feelings, and do what needs doing, seem less likely to be so distracted. We have taught these principles to adolescents who have no prior experience with such an orientation, and they have been able to use the guidelines successfully. Presumably it would be much more effective to teach decision-making with these principles from childhood, while modeling their use in daily living.

CAUTIONS

Even the simplest ideas are subject to misinterpretation and misuse; therefore a few cautions are in order regarding the application of Constructive Living ideas to parenting. First, this is not intended to be a complete system for rearing children, but to augment the effectiveness of whatever methods are already used by the parents. Some of the ideas of Constructive Living do contradict some traditional Western theories. However, the emphasis on doing what needs doing and the ideas about accepting feelings can be used in conjunction with most parenting methods if thoughtfully applied. This paper is intended to suggest some ways in which this may be done, but it seems unlikely that all ideas will be equally useful to all parents.

Second, it is a common error, in our experience, to misuse the ideas of Morita therapy to disregard feelings rather than to accept them and get on with what needs doing. As previously mentioned, we already see a number of parents who deny, rather than accept, the feelings expressed by their children, and they seem especially likely to distort their application of these ideas if not carefully guided. This distinction is often a difficult one: the intent is that the client learn to accept feelings while going on with purposeful activity; but the client often believes that if feelings are not to be the basis of action, they must be pushed aside. Acceptance is not an easy concept, either to teach or to practice.

Finally, one of the primary teachings of Constructive Living is that, in order to teach it, one must live it. This means that parents must use these principles in their own lives if they are to teach them to their children. The principle of accepting reality as it is would be especially important, because children must be accepted as they are, developmentally and individually, if they are to be parented appropriately. Neither the approaches outlined here, nor any other framework, can be applied blindly to all children in all situations. The point is that, if parents practice these principles in their own lives, they may be in a better position to teach their children how to deal with feelings and purposes less neurotically than would otherwise be possible.

CONCLUSION

Constructive Living has been taught to a number of adults and has potential applications to children as well. By modeling Constructive Living, parents may be able to provide the impetus for young people to base their behavior on purpose, with a realistic acceptance of reality, including feelings. This should produce more functional adults than either a philosophy of doing whatever one feels like at the moment or of disregarding feelings altogether.

A bit farther along the time line from childhood to adulthood we encounter the adolescent. What has Constructive Living to do with the high school student? Is there any sense in presenting a difficult, demanding lifeway to young people who are already having problems in school? Barbara Sarah and Perri Ardman present evidence from the initial phase of an ongoing program in New York. Successes and failures simply present us with more information about what needs to be done next.　　—DKR

7

CONSTRUCTIVE LIVING FOR HIGH SCHOOL STUDENTS

BARBARA SARAH AND PERRI ARDMAN

BACKGROUND

In November, 1989, the authors designed a six-week workshop in Constructive Living for teenagers who were having problems in school. The first workshop began in January, 1990, conducted by the first author. This paper briefly describes that pilot workshop and what the authors learned about using the principles of Constructive Living with low-performing high school students.

Through the practice and study of Morita principles as re-education, it became clear that the logical place to teach these principles is in the school setting. There adolescents can use the concepts to become more successful students and avoid the risks of drug and alcohol abuse and other destructive behaviors prevalent in our society today. With access to students in high school, it seemed natural to design a Constructive Living workshop for students who were having difficulty in school.

In slightly modified form this chapter was presented as a paper at the First International Congress of Morita Therapy in Hamamatsu, Japan in April, 1990. The paper was subsequently published among the proceedings of the Congress in the *Journal of Morita Therapy*, volume 1, number 2, 1990.

Five of the six workshop sessions focused heavily on teaching Morita principles.

The school administration was receptive to a program in Constructive Living, which would instruct students to take responsibility for their own efforts to become successful in school, and allowed the workshop to take place during school hours.

The students were selected according to at least one of the following criteria:

1. Students were failing two or more subjects;
2. Students were excessively absent or tardy;
3. Students were referred by school personnel;
4. Students referred themselves.

Participation in the workshop was voluntary. Thirty-three students were referred. They were all invited to attend a preview session. The session gave them an idea of what the workshop would offer and how they could benefit from it. After the preview, students decided whether or not to sign up for the six workshop sessions. Twelve of the thirty-three referred students came to the preview. Eleven of those twelve signed up for the workshop, seven girls and four boys:

Four 1st-year students, 14 years old;
Three 2nd-year students, 15 years old;
Two 3rd-year students, 16 years old;
Two 4th-year students, 17 years old.

The workshop consisted of one group-session a week for six weeks. Average attendance during the six weeks was 83 percent. Each student then had an individual session with the first author. The following week a graduation ceremony was held.

THE WORKSHOP

Each of the six workshop sessions consisted of a didactic instructional component and an experiential component.

Exercises illustrating Constructive Living concepts were conducted during the sessions, and additional assignments were to be completed between sessions.

Session One was devoted to the concepts of paying attention to reality and defining purpose.

Sessions Two and Three dealt with what is controllable (behavior), and what is not controllable (including feelings and other people).

Sessions Four and Five concentrated on appreciation, service, and the principle that effort is good fortune.

Session Six focused on how students could apply Constructive Living principles outside of school as well as in school.

The following assignments were among those given during the course:

1. Writing a Constructive Living journal;

2. Carrying out ordinary activities, like brushing teeth or washing dishes, with full attention;

3. Coming to workshop sessions even if not feeling like it;

4. Making a list of things that happened for which the students did or did not have responsibility;

5. Writing thank-you letters to school personnel;

6. Picking up trash in front of the school;

7. Doing something that needed to be done in spite of not wanting to do it;

8. Writing a letter of recommendation about themselves for the job or college they desired after high school.

RESULTS

1. First-year students with multiple course failures were unclear about their purpose for being in school. The workshop helped them to clarify their educational goals and state their desire to be more successful in their studies.

2. Students with academic problems did not know how to pay attention and live in each moment. They tended to focus

on the past—yesterday, last night, what someone told them before school, or what happened before class. Similarly, they thought about the future—what they would do after school or on the weekend. Two girls in the group admitted to spending much time in their classes thinking about what their boyfriends did or did not say to them, and what they might or might not have said back to them. Through exercises in the group and assignments during the week, they learned about living with full attention in each moment.

3. Teenagers in the workshop liked to blame their lack of success on something or someone else—the school administration or teachers, their parents, the weather and so on. They learned that only they are responsible for homework, attendance, promptness, and class participation. They were taught that they are responsible for what they do.

4. The students learned that purpose-guided actions are more effective than those guided by feelings.

5. The middle-class students in the workshop took most things in their lives for granted. Naikan principles taught of their indebtedness to others and to the world around them, a very difficult lesson.

6. The students in the workshop seemed overwhelmed by suffering, some of it needless suffering. One student, a seventeen-year-old female student, had attendance problems and anxiety about her boyfriend. She struggled during the previous year with an eating disorder. When asked if she could tell people how to suffer she wrote the following:

> Keep thinking that there's nothing good about anything. Keep remembering everything bad that's happened in your past and anyone who's treated you badly. Feel self-pity. Think about all the negative things about yourself. Think about everything negative that has happened in your life. Don't get up (in the morning). Don't leave your house. Stay home. Lock yourself in your room. Put on the most depressing music. Cry all day long. Don't talk to anyone. Don't reach out to anyone. Don't do anything productive. Just stay and sit by yourself. Don't go to school. Don't do well in school. Don't think about anything. Don't care about anything.
>
> That's how I lived my life last year.

This student distinguished herself during the workshop. She had perfect attendance, participated actively in the meetings (even though she sometimes did not feel like it), and did all of the assignments. At graduation she was awarded a workshop certificate with distinction. Constructive Living concepts had a powerful impact on this young woman. She has been accepted into the State University and will begin college in the fall.

IN CONCLUSION

Because some of the ideas of Constructive Living are so different from commonly accepted cultural perspectives, the students require more time and exposure to the concepts than occurred during only six sessions. The second workshop, in progress at this writing, will last for twelve weeks.

An outline of the weekly sessions, including exercises and homework assignments, is available from either author.

More about the broad range of Constructive Living's applications is demonstrated in this chapter. We are presented with information about the life problems of a special suffering population. HIV+ victims are special, yet not special. Their distress looks like ours. Their utilization of CL principles inspires us. Gregory Willms kindly presents us with a glimpse of the challenges and hardships of this patient population. He demonstrates that suffering can become transcendence.   —DKR

8

MORITA'S PRINCIPLES AND HIV INFECTION

GREGORY WILLMS

Since the mid-eighties my psychotherapy practice has come to include an increasing number of clients who are affected by the AIDS epidemic. They include people who carry, or fear that they carry, the human immunodeficiency virus, HIV, and are currently healthy; people who have been diagnosed with AIDS and are living in various states of health and disease; people whose lives are ending; and people whose partners, friends, or family members are threatened, sick, or have died as a result of HIV infection.

My purpose in this work has been to be of some help or use to the people involved. I am more certain, however, that these clients have served as my teachers. Clearly, the assumptions and techniques of the psychotherapies in which I had originally been trained were insufficient to deal with these compelling realities. More and more I found myself looking to the situations themselves, rather than to theory, for my information on what needed to be done.

In slightly modified form this chapter was presented as a paper at the First International Congress of Morita Therapy in Hamamatsu, Japan in April, 1990. The paper was subsequently published among the proceedings of the Congress in the *Journal of Morita Therapy*, volume 1, number 2, 1990.

Through the writings of Constructive Living, and later through training in Constructive Living, I had the good fortune to be introduced to the work of Dr. Shoma Morita. I found Moritist thought to be a clear articulation of psychological principles which fit my own experience and that of my clients.

In general, most of my clients come to therapy to fix or change what they feel. In the case of HIV infection, this desire is frequently compounded by certain currently popular beliefs and theories that view "positive" feelings as promoting health, and "negative" feelings like sadness, grief, and anger as contributing to and even causing disease. A major portion of the therapy I do has the purpose of teaching and reminding the client that they are not responsible for their feelings, that their feelings are not directly controllable by their will, and that feelings can be simply recognized and accepted as they are.

One client came to me in rapidly declining health three years after being diagnosed with AIDS. Two months earlier he had been hospitalized in a psychiatric facility for what was described as a psychotic break. He subsequently continued to avoid therapeutic help, afraid that he was indeed crazy. After he was finally pressured into seeing me, my initial intervention was to clarify that not only were his fears of sickness and death uncontrollable, they were completely natural under the circumstances; it would be the lack of such fear that might cause me to question his sanity. "In Morita's view the basic fear of all humans is death. Fear of illness is rooted in this fear of death. Morita believed that no one can avoid the fear and sorrow associated with dying" (Reynolds, 1986, p.87). This client came to accept the naturalness of his fear, and in the process, forgot his concern with going insane—the suffering on top of his suffering. In this acceptance, the client also realized that even the most difficult of his feelings had its uses.

In particular, as he accepted his fear of death he found it to be inseparable from his desire to live, and to live fully—what Morita called *sei no yokubo*. The client quite naturally turned his attention from his feelings to the things that needed to be done in his life. As the organist of a major cathedral, he had written a large amount of liturgical music over the years. He organized this music and sent it to a university library where it would continue to be played. As his health declined, he sorted through his furniture and belongings, giving them away to the appropriate friends, family members, and charities. When finally confined to bed, he acted the part of host for his visitors, concerning himself with his guests' comfort, the arrangement of the pictures and flowers in the room, and the offering of cookies, tea, and coffee. He was particularly interested in the personal connections that could be made while he was dying, so he arranged simultaneous visits during which he introduced his family, friends, and health care providers to each other. When exhausted, he would choose the restaurant most appropriate for the people visiting him, call to make reservations, and send them on their way.

I find that the heart of working with HIV-infected people is really the same as working with any others—while accepting things as they are, *arugamama*, one "pays attention and acts purposefully" (Reynolds, 1984, p. 92). Again and again it seems vital to distinguish what can be controlled and what cannot, and to act on what can be controlled. Some examples may be useful here. One client came to therapy because of extreme anxiety over his HIV infection, though he was currently in good health. While slowly accepting his fear of a potentially fatal condition, he turned his attention and effort to volunteer work, massaging people with AIDS at the local community hospital. Another client had been a small-town parish priest when he was hospitalized for pneumonia and diagnosed with AIDS. On learning of his condition he abruptly left town. In therapy he came to accept not only his fear of death, but also his fear of his congregation's judgment. He recognized the need to return to his church, where he preached a farewell sermon and met with concerned parishioners. Still another client, though struggling with exhaustion, continued his internship at a correctional facility for juvenile offenders and completed his degree in counseling. In each of these cases, the focus became that of purposeful action. This resolve was particularly apparent in a client who was faced with having to discontinue either a medication which prevented his going blind or a medication which helped to maintain his fragile health. Since he was involved in the final stages of building a home for himself and his partner, he kept his sight and was able to finish the home shortly before his death.

I regularly work with clients in three basic areas of daily living and health: eating, sleeping, and exercise. For example, one client was steadily losing weight. He attributed this weight loss to his lack of energy to cook for himself, his lack of interest in the food others prepared for him, and his lack of a sense of taste (a side effect of his medications). I made it clear to him that from my point of view he was not dying of AIDS, he was starving himself to death. He agreed to go through his cookbooks, listing any foods that attracted him. He shopped from this list, and shared it with his friends and family who even used Air Express to ship him poke salad, a green vegetable popular in the South. After he began to recover both weight and health he invited me to his home for a dinner he had made of Southern fried chicken, mashed potatoes and gravy, biscuits, poke salad, and pie.

As Morita pointed out, the practice of attention is the essential foundation for a reality-based life. In teaching this I have been helped greatly by the birds who come to the feeder outside my office window. One client in particular wanted to use his time in a recitation of the harshness and injustice of his life, only to be repeatedly distracted by the variety of birds hopping by the window. It was important to ask him where his suffering was when he was watching the birds.

I returned from a training session to find another client just home after a second hospitalization for pneumonia. Rather than focus all of our attention on his recent struggle, I invited him to a gentle hike in the hills to see the spring wildflowers. He agreed, and later described his experience as being much like his transformative encounters with psychedelic drugs as a younger man. Though his comparison may seem curious, it clearly points to his experience of the deep power of attending to reality moment by moment.

Another young man was hospitalized, probably for the last time. In his hospital room, we began to list all that was contributing to his living at that moment. He included the nurse on call, the geysers that provided electricity for the lights, electronic monitors of his physiological condition, and air conditioning, the AIDS activists who had pressured for the release of the drug he was receiving, the steady beating of his heart, his parents who had come from Maryland to be with him, etc.. So clearly, in this noticing he lived his life while alive.

Constructive Living expresses certain of Morita's principles with the saying "nothing special." This is particularly helpful for people with HIV infection. Especially due to strong identification with their sexuality or with their drug use, many have cultivated the particular suffering that comes with specialness. With HIV, many feel singled out again as special cases. Certainly, all of these feelings must be accepted as they are. Equally, it must be recognized and accepted that sickness, old age, and death (even if premature) are nothing special. They are a natural part of ordinary human life. And for all of us not-so-special human beings, the real question is one of attention and purposeful action in each moment.

Again, I want to express my gratitude to all of these people for sharing with me the rich realities of their lives; to Dr. Shoma Morita and those who have followed him in his work for their clear thinking and skillful means; and to Dr. David Reynolds for bringing these principles and this practice to the United States.

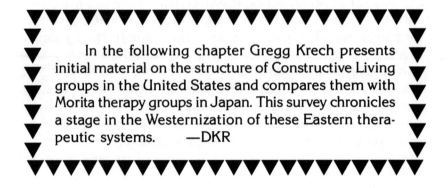
In the following chapter Gregg Krech presents initial material on the structure of Constructive Living groups in the United States and compares them with Morita therapy groups in Japan. This survey chronicles a stage in the Westernization of these Eastern therapeutic systems.   —DKR

9

EXPLORING GROUP MODELS FOR TEACHING THE PRINCIPLES OF CONSTRUCTIVE LIVING

GREGG KRECH

Morita therapy, initially developed in Japan by the psychiatrist Shoma Morita (1874–1938), was first introduced in the United States shortly after World War II. In more recent years, largely through the work of Dr. David Reynolds (1976, 1980, 1984, 1989), there has been a growing interest in Morita therapy. The publication of sixteen books on the subject and more than a dozen professional journal and magazine articles by Reynolds, creation of a national newsletter, ongoing workshops, public talks, and professional training have served to introduce many Westerners to an alternative to traditional Western therapies. Reynolds has combined the principles and treatment methods of Morita therapy with those of Naikan (Reynolds, 1983), another form of Japanese psychotherapy, resulting in a therapeutic method and way of life referred to as Constructive Living.

The rapid growth of Morita therapy in the past five years has resulted in the recent development of Morita and Constructive Living groups in several metropolitan areas of the United States. Such groups operate with norms, methods, and assumptions very different from traditional Western therapy groups. To date, no research has been conducted on the nature of these groups, the way they operate, the characteristics of participants and leaders, on the outcomes achieved. This chapter is an effort to present an initial study of five such groups and to create a foundation for further research related to issues affecting methods and outcomes of this group model.

METHOD

Subjects of the study are adult males and females who have participated in at least one group meeting in any of the cities selected for study. The cities of Washington, D.C., New York, Chicago, Los Angeles, and San Francisco all have active groups with group leaders trained by Reynolds. A questionnaire was designed to solicit information on participants' background, occupation, purpose of attendance, and perception of leader's style. Questionnaires were sent to a total of forty-four group-participants in the five selected cities. Questionnaires were distributed by group leaders and returned directly to the author of this paper.

Additional data were collected from the group leader in each city through telephone interviews to determine group methods of operation and to compare the leaders' views with those of the participants. The author was the group leader for the Washington, D.C. and New York groups at the time of this study.

RESULTS AND DISCUSSION

Participant Background

Thirty-six respondents returned completed questionnaires for a return rate of approximately 82 percent. The resulting sample included 18 male and 18 female participants. The mean age of group participants was 42.2 years, ranging from the youngest participant of 26 years to the oldest of 65. When sorted by city, Los Angeles had the highest mean age of 48, while New York had the lowest mean age of 37. All but one of the respondents were Caucasian.

The occupations of the respondents varied greatly, though they were overwhelmingly engaged in white-collar jobs. Medical and mental health clinicians made up the largest segment of the sample (22 percent), while writers/editors were also disproportionally represented (11 percent). Most of the remaining participants were engaged in either business activities or the arts, having achieved some reasonable status as determined by their stated occupational titles. These data would support the hypothesis that those involved in Morita/CL groups have achieved some significant career success, though they may still be searching for some therapeutic or philosophical approach to help them live better or handle personal problems.

An overwhelming majority of the respondents (87 percent) had been in some type of therapy prior to becoming involved with Morita and Constructive Living. Forty-five percent of the respondents had engaged in individual Morita therapy or Constructive Living instruction prior to, or concurrently with, group participation. However, when the groups are considered separately, the Chicago and Los Angeles groups have much lower percentages of "concurrent participants" (17 percent and 20 percent) than the other three cities. None of the surveyed therapists/instructors either required or precluded concurrent participation in the local group for individual students/clients. Such participation was always the choice of the student, and the author is aware of several individuals who chose not to participate in groups. Group students who were also engaged in individual therapy had an average of seven individual sessions each at the time of the survey.

Morita-Based Groups in Japan

Seikatsu no Hakkenkai (HK) is a Morita-based mental health organization in Japan that was established in 1971 to support and promote group-based Morita therapy among the Japanese. A 1987 survey revealed that HK had 5,437 members and had established 101 regional groups (called *shudankai*) throughout Japan (Hasegawa, 1988). Each group is attended by 10–30 individuals. Most HK members exhibit symptoms of neurosis including obsessive-compulsive disorders, social phobia and anxiety neuroses. Traditionally, Morita therapy has been narrowly applied as a treatment for *shinkeishitsu*, a condition characterized by symptoms of self-preoccupation such as obsessive shyness, oversensitivity, and feelings of inferiority (Reynolds, 1976). However, some modern Japanese clinicians appear to be broadening the application of Morita therapy, and Kora has noted that it can produce useful results in treating other psychiatric problems if applied together with other forms of treatment (Kora, 1989).

The *shudankai* groups are led by senior members who have completed a standard course in Morita theory. New members are often paired with more experienced members in a system similar to Alcoholics Anonymous and other self-help groups in the United States. Meetings may begin with participants introducing themselves and then proceed to an exchange of personal experiences and group study of Morita theory. Participants set goals for the coming month and then report their progress at the next meeting. According to Hasegawa, group participation results in the following benefits:

1. Members realize they are not alone in their suffering and are accepted by fellow members;

2. Members are able to view their symptoms more objectively by learning about others' symptoms;

3. Members have an opportunity to give and receive mutual help and encouragement;

4. Members renew their hope of, and confidence in, getting better;

5. Members are able to refocus their attention on healthier and more realistic interests in living.

The *shudankai* meetings continue for three to four hours and use the key elements of Morita theory in order to educate members to take constructive action in the face of unpleasant feelings. The concept of *arugamama* (accepting feelings as they are) is emphasized as members learn that they cannot control their feelings, but that they can act constructively regardless of how they are feeling. Members are also taught that their attention has become fixated on their subjective symptoms and that the shifting of attention can provide relief from much of their neurosis-based suffering.

Morita and Constructive Living Groups in the United States

The Morita and Constructive Living groups which are now operating in the United States are in some respects similar to their Japanese counterparts and in other ways quite different. No national organization exists in the United States, although there is a loose association and network of therapists and instructors who have trained under Reynolds. The first group began in Los Angeles in 1981 and was led by Reynolds. The group disbanded in 1983 and was reorganized in 1989 by a former student. The remaining four groups used in the study were all founded in 1988 or 1989. Membership in local groups is somewhat smaller than in *shudankai* with most meetings being attended by 6–12 individuals. The majority of group members (51 percent) received information about the group from either mailings or by word-of-mouth.

Unlike the Japanese, participants do not share a clinical symptomology which attracts them to these groups. Morita's principles are applied broadly and seen as useful guidelines for a constructive approach to life, regardless of the specific nature of a person's suffering. Difficulties in life regarding intimate relationships, career choices, money, health, and family are experienced by most of us at one point or another, as are the affective responses of fear, anger, depression, shyness, and anxiety. The principles of Morita therapy provide a basis for accepting feelings and responding to life's difficulties in a constructive manner. The following list of principles, taken from a paper distributed to group members in Washington, D.C. (Krech, 1988), provides an example of the underlying assumptions used to conduct this group:

1. Our feelings and thoughts are uncontrollable directly by our will. Every feeling, no matter how unpleasant, has its uses. Unpleasant feelings often provide a basis

for making changes and accomplishing things that might not otherwise occur.

2. Our feelings can be indirectly influenced by changes in our behavior and environment.

3. We should learn to recognize and accept all feelings rather than resist or try to change them.

4. It is possible to respond to each situation constructively regardless of how we are feeling. Our feelings do not control our behavior.

5. Inward attention and fixation on our inner-experience prolongs suffering. Outward attention provides a basis for knowing what needs to be done and allows us to experience life fully.

The above statements about feelings appear consistent with the principles used in the HK groups. However, there is a noticeable absence of any discussion of the *shinkeishitsu* symptoms which are emphasized by the Japanese (Ohara, Fujita, Kora). These statements about feelings can be traced to the Japanese writings of respected Morita therapists. For example, one can compare the fifth statement above to the following comment by Koga (1967):

"Agonies appear and anxieties flourish when a person becomes overly egocentric and knowingly (or unknowingly) directs his mind to himself. On the other hand, unexpected elevation and development of one's self becomes possible when the mind is taken off from one's self and directed to the surrounding."

Similar comparisons can be made between many of the assumptions and principles used in the U.S. groups and those used clinically by the Japanese. This is to be expected since the U.S. groups can all be traced to Reynolds, who was trained by, and has worked closely with, Japanese psychiatrists for the past twenty-five years.

The format for groups in the United States varies slightly from city to city. A general description of the format for the Washington, D.C. group would be as follows:

The group usually begins by participants briefly introducing themselves and then reporting on their major accomplishments for the past month. In some cases these reports may include instances in which Morita principles have been used and adapted to particular situations. The second phase of the group involves a lecture and discussion of some particular principle of Morita or Naikan. The discussion can be lively with participants either challenging the leader or one another. The lecture phase is generally conducted by the group leader, although from time to time a guest speaker will be brought in to address the group. This might be a visiting Morita therapist or, in one case, a teacher of the Japanese tea ceremony. In the final phase, there is open discussion and questions. "Here and Now" exercises may be given without warning, such as inviting the group members to close their eyes and describe the clothes other participants are wearing. Such exercises serve to reinforce Morita principles (paying attention to surroundings, in this case) in the present moment and remind group members that the meetings themselves are simply another occasion to practice the application of these principles to daily life. Prior to the close of the meeting, new monthly goals for each member are developed which are both specific and controllable. Finally, assignments and exercises are suggested which participants may carry out before the next meeting.

The following elements exist, to a greater or lesser degree, in all of the U.S. Morita and Constructive Living groups:

1. There is an emphasis on what people are doing, rather than how they are feeling; efforts are directed toward constructive action in life rather than toward feeling better;

2. The group leader is viewed primarily as a teacher—someone who has a basic understanding of these principles in daily life and can teach others methods which can improve the way the students live. The group leader generally makes some type of didactic presentation during the meeting. The presentation leads to discussion and questions;

3. There is a focus on the personal and direct experience of participants rather than on theoretical issues;

4. Exercises and assignments to be carried out both during the meeting and prior to the following meeting are designed to teach the principles of Morita and Naikan;

5. The use of readings, books, handouts, and articles to support more direct learning methods is encouraged.

Another way in which U.S. groups contrast with their Japanese counterparts is the inclusion of Naikan principles and exercises. Respondents in four of the five groups viewed Naikan as comprising 40–45 percent of the group time. Only in the Chicago group was Naikan less emphasized, primarily due to the newness of the group. The Chicago group focused heavily on Morita in its first set of meetings. Naikan's reflective emphasis on the specific support one receives seems to comfortably complement the directness and action-oriented principles of Morita. Group leaders reported no significant conflicts in utilizing both therapeutic models.

When respondents were asked what "style" most accurately described the group leader, 56 percent chose "teacher" while 33 percent chose "facilitator." Only 6 percent viewed the group leader's style as that of a "therapist". Given the high percentage of participants who had some type of prior therapy (87 percent), we can conclude that the style of group leaders contrasts significantly with that of the Western therapists to whom respondents had been exposed. Indeed, many elements of Morita and Constructive Living groups would seem to indicate that the approach is more educational than it is therapeutic. The use of assignments (homework), the perceived style of the group leader, the absence of efforts to "work on" feelings, the didactic presentations, and use of readings and handouts—all have a strong educational flavor to them. When respondents were asked what elements of the group were most important to them, educationally oriented items such as "questions and discussion with others," "receiving assignments," and "information from the group's leader" were most often ranked first or second while items such as "group support and encouragement" were perceived as far less important.

Morita himself clearly viewed his method of helping people as educational, calling it "re-education." Koga (1967) states that:

> ". . . Professor Morita constantly reminded us that those to whom the treatment is administered are not patients in the strict sense of the word, that it is not befitting to call them patients at all in the light of his theory, and that the most appropriate term for the so-called treatment is 're-education.' "

Educationally based groups are not new to the West, though they do not fit the common stereotypes of groups as being intimate and oriented towards "sharing feelings." Klapman (1950) developed a didactic group therapy for outpatients, which included formal lectures and textbook assignments. Marsh (1935) created a classroom setting by means of lectures, homework, and grading. Malamud and Machover (1965) organized "workshops in self-understanding" composed of patients taken from a waiting list of a psychiatric clinic. The goal was to prepare patients for group psychotherapy. At the conclusion of fifteen two-hour modules, many patients felt sufficiently improved so that no further treatment was required.

CONCLUSION

Morita therapy is one of the most important therapeutic methods practiced in Japan. There group models flourish as a key methodology for helping people who suffer from a form of neurosis called *shinkeishitsu*. The growing popularity of Morita therapy in the United States has resulted in the formation of similar groups in several metropolitan areas. While the U.S. groups have adopted the same fundamental therapeutic principles as their Japanese counterparts, they have also incorporated the principles of Naikan psychotherapy and rely heavily on the group leader as a teacher or instructor of these principles. The U.S. groups have assumed a broader application of such principles as a way of life rather than as a clinical treatment narrowly directed toward a well-defined set of neurotic symptoms. These groups employ an educationally based model that bears little resemblance to most Western therapeutic approaches. This model is viewed by proponents as training and education rather than therapy. Research in the efficacy of Morita therapy as a clinical treatment for neurosis indicates a high rate of success in Japan (Yokoyama, 1968) (Suzuki, 1967) (Ohara, Aizawa and Iwai, 1970). However, no outcome-oriented research is available in the United States regarding individual or group-based models of Morita therapy in its expanded form. Such research would contribute much to documenting the efficacy of these methods to Westerners. Future research should examine the level of effectiveness of Morita-based principles in the broader context of human suffering.

CONSTRUCTIVE LIVING
AND BUSINESS

Constructive Living principles are readily applied to the world of business. What has CL to contribute to the workplace? When one considers that many people spend long hours of their everyday lives in the workplace it becomes clear that any overall life strategy cannot afford to ignore applications to business. Mary J. Puckett presents an introduction to this area of high potential.   —DKR

10

CONSTRUCTIVE LIVING AND BUSINESS

MARY J. PUCKETT

Constructive Living is a program for getting things done. The best motivational technique is doing things rather than planning, talking, or getting ready to do them, according to psychological anthropologist David Reynolds. "Don't greet someone with, 'How are you feeling?'; greet him with, 'How are you doing?'" he advises. Reynolds developed Constructive Living with an orientation to action based on purpose and ethical choice rather than on feelings.

Gregg Krech consults with businesses in several countries from his office in Arlington, Virginia. Since beginning to work with Reynolds several years ago, he has used both Morita and Naikan in his approach to organizational development. He believes Constructive Living is more practical, and more acceptable to businesses, than the traditional approaches.

"Organizational development usually has been very feeling-focused, with T-groups and similar methods that emphasize personal relationships within the company," he points out. "There has been a lot of resistance to this emphasis on feelings from some managers, and there should be, because all that isn't necessary."

The focus in Constructive Living is on tasks that need doing, and everyone focuses on the tasks of the organization. Krech says:

"The purpose of my consultation is to develop organizational behavior built on Morita and Naikan principles so that the individuals in the organization have an attitude of wanting to support the company and the people in it."

Everyone needs to use this approach, from the CEO down, he points out. "When each individual works this way, the organization runs well because everyone is giving one hundred percent."

Instead of getting people from a division together to talk about their feelings, Krech assigns them action-oriented tasks. One typical assignment is to spend an hour during the day doing someone else's job in the division. "This provides an experience of service to others, as well as knowledge of what another person's work is like," he says.

A one-time exercise like this has a limited effect, but the principles of appreciation for others through doing, rather than talking or feeling, can change an entire corporate culture if applied over a period of time. "Naikan helps you look at the ways in which you're constantly supported by others as you go through your day," Krech says. The Constructive Living emphasis is on what you can do for other people and on appreciation for the things they do for you.

Morita is action-oriented. In every moment there is something that needs to be done. Looking carefully at the current situation, with a view to one's purpose in it, will reveal what needs doing. However, to get a clear view, it is necessary to accept one's feelings without being sidetracked by them. Morita teaches the skills necessary to do this.

One of the important points from Morita is that people are only responsible for their own behavior, regardless of how they feel. A corollary is that they cannot control the behavior of others. "I suggest that people focus on what they can do, rather than what others should do. It's a much more productive approach," Krech says. He points out, patiently and repeatedly, that the best results are obtained in a company when all team members take full responsibility for doing their best and focus on their own performance rather than judging others. When implemented, this viewpoint reduces the often-heard complaint that some co-workers are "not doing their share."

The Naikan aspect of Constructive Living teaches an appreciation of the many ways in which we are supported by the world. It provides a global view of how all things are related to each other. A businessman learns to see that he is supported by the help of his office staff, by the customers who make up his business, by his suppliers, the people who pick up his trash, the waiter who serves his lunch, and many others. The view provides a different way of getting through the day than the more common idea that we are owed these services and that the people providing them probably should be doing a better job.

The president of one of the companies with which Krech has consulted was known as a man who spoke to his employees primarily when there were problems. On one occasion he and Krech had dinner shortly before a working holiday, Valentine's Day. Krech suggested that on the upcoming holiday the president give each staff member a rose and a thank-you note for some specific job well done. Although skeptical, the president finally agreed and implemented the plan, with assistance from Krech on the content of the notes. Most employees were surprised and pleased with the thanks, though Krech says the point is that the president needed to express thanks as much as the employees needed to receive it.

Krech points out several things to be learned from this experience. It is the president's responsibility to express appreciation because he is supported by his employees, whether or not they respond well to his offers. Over time, such gratitude will set up a business environment that will encourage workers to express appreciation to each other and to customers, with probable improvements in job performance and sales. One such gesture may not make a lasting change, but gratitude expressed repeatedly over time will have a positive influence on most people in the workplace. "People want to work and do a good job for someone who is appreciative," Krech points out.

Of course, it is the function of the manager to be responsible for the work of subordinates, and to evaluate that work. Krech instructs supervisors how to use the principles of Constructive Living, and how to teach them to subordinates, as part of a plan to improve performance. He points out, however, that recognition of others' efforts (and the gratitude that often accompanies such recognition) is one of the most effective tools available to management.

One company with which Krech has consulted is Laboratories pro Salud, a Mexican division of Merck Sharp & Dohme. Krech spent three days in Mexico teaching Constructive Living principles. The company hopes this instruction will help personnel make the most of their work-lives. The emphasis was not on the company or the division, but on what each individual can accomplish. "Everyone has a certain amount of time before leaving a particular job," Krech points out. "The key question is, what does he want to accomplish in that time? What does he want to leave as his legacy?" Krech and Jesus Zamora, the manager who invited him to Laboratories pro Salud, want to focus on long-term contributions, not just getting through each day. They believe that helping each employee make his best contribution will have a beneficial effect on the division.

Phil Saperstein, vice-president of technical services for Modine Manufacturing, also believes Constructive Living has a future in business. "I got involved in Constructive Living for myself," he says, "but it connects to a number of things we do to help the company."

One of Saperstein's innovations is an annual appreciation banquet, to which anyone who has submitted an idea for technical innovation is invited. "The intent was nothing more than to say 'thank you,'" he says, "but we got more than we bargained for." Ideas for technical innovation have increased threefold since the banquet was implemented. Such a dramatic increase is important in an industry that depends on technical innovation for its survival. Although there was some initial difficulty in convincing others of the importance of public appreciation, the banquet has been a success.

What are the benefits of Constructive Living for business? Reynolds and Krech report that most people who go through

Constructive Living training develop a more service-oriented attitude, and have more self-management tools to accomplish their purpose.

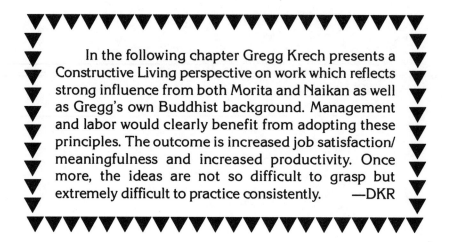

In the following chapter Gregg Krech presents a Constructive Living perspective on work which reflects strong influence from both Morita and Naikan as well as Gregg's own Buddhist background. Management and labor would clearly benefit from adopting these principles. The outcome is increased job satisfaction/ meaningfulness and increased productivity. Once more, the ideas are not so difficult to grasp but extremely difficult to practice consistently.   —DKR

11

DOING A GOOD JOB: CONSTRUCTIVE LIVING GUIDELINES FOR LIFE AT WORK

GREGG KRECH

Constructive Living offers practical principles to help guide us to a more meaningful life. It is equally relevant to our work. Of course, work is just another element of life. Now we're at home, now we're at work. Now we're with our family, now we're with our colleagues. Life is just life. So we must do our best to live well regardless of where we are or what we're doing. Constructive Living contains wisdom derived from the direct experience of life. This wisdom points us in the direction of living well. So, actually, it is life that teaches us how to live. Similarly, it is life that teaches us how to work. Here are some basic guidelines for living well at work. These suggestions for living well apply not only to the place of employment; they are just as relevant to cooking dinner for your family or fixing your washing machine.

WORK IS DONE FOR ITS OWN SAKE

Are you working to get rich? So you can retire? So you can get a promotion? So you can become better at what you do? So you can get recognition from others? Whatever else you have in mind, work should be done because it needs to be done. The work deserves your attention. You may or may not be rewarded for your effort. If you are working solely for reward and recognition, you may occasionally be frustrated and resentful. If you are working solely in order to be happy, you face some measure of disappointment. If you are working just so you can enjoy the weekend, you risk wasting your life in between the weekends. But if you are working in order to do the work; then your primary task is to do your best. What more can you do? Reynolds translates Morita's maxim "*Doryoku sunawachi Kofuku*" as "Effort is good fortune". It is our effort which is truly important. Just doing the work is good fortune. Just having work to do is good fortune. If there were no work to do, what would we do? So Constructive Living recommends that you do each task, each project as if it were the last thing you will do before you die. Put your whole life into it. Every moment you have lived has been training for this. . .and now this. . .and now this. . .

DOING WHAT NEEDS TO BE DONE

The nature of most organizations is that each person has job responsibilities. Sometimes the responsibilities are clear, sometimes ambiguous. Sometimes people's duties overlap. Regardless of how the workplace is structured each person is responsible for what he or she needs to do. So it is important that work be handled responsibly and in a timely manner. This is often our objective, though our optimal performance may be lacking at times.

Here is a suggestion which may surprise you: I recommend that you do other peoples' work as well as your own when circumstances warrant lending a hand. It's both absurd and selfish to think that we are paid to do only our own job.

Consider a football team. Each player has an assignment for each play. Let's say your assignment is to block a particular player who is trying to tackle your quarterback. You succeed, but then you notice that another opposing player is running past you and is about to crush your quarterback. There is nobody else who can block him but you. Do you do it? Of course. What's the point of succeeding in your assignment if the fundamental purpose of the team is not accomplished? So when there is an opportunity to help someone else do their work, it is your responsibility to do so. If you have a trashcan next to your desk and there is a garbage bin in the parking lot, why not empty your trash on the way to your car?

If you are caught up in the idea of rigid organizational charts and tight job descriptions, then this recommendation may sound confusing. But if you can see that it is not *your* work or *their* work but *the* work which needs doing, then the counsel makes more sense. Forget your formal job title. Make it your specialty to be just doing what needs to be done.

IF I DON'T DO IT NOW, WHEN ELSE CAN I DO IT?

When the Zen Master Dogen Zenji was in China in the year 1223 he met an old monk who was the cook at a Zen monastery. The old man was out in the vegetable garden, covered with sweat. His eyebrows were white and his feet burned from walking on tiles scorched by the summer sun. Dogen Zenji watched him working to gather vegetables for the evening meal. He then asked, "Why are you working so hard under the heat of an afternoon sun?" The monk replied, "If I do not do it now, when else can I do it?"

What more could be said? The monk did not delay his work because of the sun, or his feelings, or his mood that afternoon. He taught Dogen that the only time something can be done is right now. So always ask yourself what is it that is most important to do right now? Lives reflect priorities. Priorities are not lists of words; they can be deduced from the use of time. There is no procrastination. There is only what is being done right now, and everything else that is not being done. The saying "I'll do this task later" refers to something that cannot be. It is impossible to do anything later. There is only this precious moment which is now our lives.

Student: "But there are so many things to be done. How can I know what is most important right now?"

Reynolds: "How did you know you should ask that question?"

PAYING ATTENTION

When we are doing something, it is important to immerse ourselves in the pursuit completely. That means focusing all of our attention on what we are doing. Many of us have had experiences of being so deeply engrossed in an activity that we lost track of everything else. Time passed unnoticed and even the "I" that was doing the job went unnoticed. In these moments we disappeared into our work. But it is not always possible to focus our attention so perfectly because our minds will often wander with distracting thoughts, feelings, and sounds. What can be done in such situations?

Our minds can be compared to a television set. We begin working on some task and that task is on a particular channel. But the tuner on the television has a tendency to fade into other stations. Before we know it we're thinking about what we're going to do later tonight (perhaps that's our entertainment channel); so we bring our attention back to our project, but then suddenly we realize we're watching "Concerns About Our Health" which is on yet another channel. So, once again, we turn back to our project, and, after some time, the channel changes again. It's not that our mental television set is broken, this operation is normal. All we can do is continue to bring our attention back to the channel for what we're doing. The real challenge is to notice that the channel has changed and to return to the proper station as quickly as possible.

There are several reasons for paying attention to what you are doing. First, when you are absorbed in your work you are not absorbed in any unpleasant thoughts and feelings. So attention to work helps to provide a distraction, a temporary respite, from suffering, particularly during periods when those thoughts and feelings are very painful. Second, you are less likely to make mistakes; so the quality of your work is likely to be better. Third, attending to reality tells us what we need to do. By paying attention your interest and curiosity may be stimulated. You may notice a better way to do the job or improve a product. Finally, I will suggest that living with full attention is simply a better way of life. Reynolds states that "training to fully focus one's attention results not in a normal life, but a superior one." When we truly open our senses to life around us it comes alive. It breathes and dances in living color. We cannot replicate such vivid experience merely by thinking or imagining it.

OTHERS ARE NOT CONTROLLABLE

Notice the difference between the following two sets of statements.

Group A

"He shouldn't talk about other people behind their backs."

"She always takes an extra half-hour for lunch."

"He thinks he knows everything. He never listens to anyone's suggestions."

"She's so negative. She's always complaining."

Group B

"I need to be more careful with respect to my talking about others."

"I'm going to start arriving at these meetings on time."

"I'm going to listen more and talk less at the staff meeting."

"I need to recycle all this wasted paper."

Some people spend a lot of time and attention "working on" the lives of their co-workers. What are the results of these efforts? Occasionally others change in the direction we desire. Yet we may continue to criticize, judge and complain. As a result we may stimulate feelings of frustration and resentment. We experience the powerlessness that comes with trying to change what isn't controllable. Even as we try to change others, we end up changing ourselves. It's more efficient just to work on our own lives directly.

There is no shortage of improvements I can make in the way I'm living and working. On any given day there is an abundance of acts I can perform to improve what I do and how I'm doing it. Of course, that takes effort. It's easier to notice changes others need to make than to actually act on changes I need to make in my life. In any case, I increase the likelihood that I'll have an influence on others by living well myself. Few are the supervisors who are truly modeling the behavior they wish from their subordinates. The best way to teach other people is by example.

Of course it is proper to support and help others when possible, but we cannot control the behavior of other human beings. We taught this lesson to our parents, and we've learned it from our children. Only what *we* do is controllable.

DOING GRATITUDE

Consider all that you receive in order to do your job. Your work is probably supported in many concrete ways by the people and things around you. Just look about you. Someone made those tools and products you use. Someone packaged and delivered them. Walk around your workplace. Look at the people and things that have helped you do your job. Notice how much more difficult your work would be without your chair, a telephone, your clients or customers, the bathroom.

Does this exercise seem awkward or strange? We may not be accustomed to noticing the variety of ways we're being supported. There is a Zen saying, "When the shoe fits, we forget the foot". Of course, when our car breaks down we immediately realize how much easier life is with a car that gets us wherever we want to go whenever we want to go there. But when our car is running well, day after day, we may pay little attention to it. Instead, our attention is more likely on other things like the problems and difficulties others are causing us. It is a valuable exercise to notice the practical contributions to our lives made by cars, clients, co-workers, and other aspects of our world. It is also valuable to actually express appreciation for them.

It is not necessary to feel grateful for what is received. The feeling of gratitude will come and go on its own. But we can do gratitude, feeling like it or not: We can thank people verbally; we can write thank you notes and give people small gifts as an expression of our appreciation; we can make other special efforts to do something in return for what we have received. These are ways in which we "do gratitude." Doing gratitude has the effect of changing things. The experience of work changes as we notice all that we are receiving and focus less on all the problems and effort. We come to realize how much of what we previously considered to be our own accomplishment belongs to others, as well. In reality, we belong to a team, even though we may not have felt like team members. Doing gratitude may sometimes stimulate the feeling of gratitude. But acts of support and service deserve our thanks anyway.

Some people believe that it's not necessary to express thanks aloud. "Why thank someone when they're only doing what they're being paid to do anyway?" In other cases people suggest that their appreciation is always understood by others so it is a waste of time to actually express it. How should one respond to such viewpoints? Perhaps by thanking such people for their advice.

REFLECTING ON TROUBLES CAUSED

Most people look in a mirror at least once each day. The mirror helps us put on makeup or comb our hair. We can check to see if anything is out of place before we leave the house. The mirror serves an important purpose. Without it, we would have great difficulty knowing if something needed to be fixed or changed. Those around us have no trouble seeing us, but we need the assistance of a mirror. We also need to take the time to look and to be willing to see what needs to be changed beyond our personal appearance.

When we look at the ways in which we are causing difficulties or troubles to others, we open ourselves to constructive changes in the way we work and relate to them. We give ourselves an opportunity to serve and support the efforts of others instead of being completely engulfed by the self-centered concerns of our own projects and goals. Part of our job becomes making other people's jobs easier. One of our goals becomes the support of our co-workers' goals. In order to be truly supportive, we must take an honest look at how we are causing difficulty to them. When consulting, I frequently hear the comment, "I wish he would just leave me alone and let me do my job." We may see how other people are making our work more difficult and wish they would see it, too. But to others, we may be one of those people making their work more difficult.

Why should we be concerned with supporting the work efforts of others and causing less trouble? Why not just put all our effort into reaching our own goals? If we should step on their toes, well, that's their problem. Once we begin to see all the support we are receiving from others we may naturally want to offer them assistance in return. A friend of mine reflected on how important the contribution of her organization's accountant has been. She realized that the respectable quality of their finances was a direct result of this person's skill and effort. Her immediate, and natural, response was to take him to lunch to show him her appreciation. Our desire to support others may come from recognition of the ways they have supported us.

Most of us want to do a good job. We want to be seen as competent and responsible. We want to be the kind of person others want to have around. But to become competent, we would do well to look at areas where we are incompetent. To become responsible, we might look at areas where we are irresponsible. If we want to be a positive force in our organization, we must be able to see ways in which we have been a negative force. We may feel guilty. Guilt isn't necessarily to be avoided. Guilt may accompany a message indicating we need to change, to act differently. Guilt comes from a desire to do well. We can nurture this healthy desire by making constructive changes in our work and life. We can thus unlock a door allowing us to move further toward fulfilling life's potential.

CHOOSING CONSTRUCTIVE WORK

This principle deals with a fundamental aspect of our work—the choice of what work we do. We are born. We spend much of our life working. And then we die. So this is truly an important choice. In large part, our work will reflect the purpose for which we have lived. Many people rightly struggle with the choice of a vocation. It's not a choice to be made lightly.

I believe we should choose work which is constructive. By constructive, I mean work which makes a contribution to others and the world in which we live. Constructive work means work which moves toward the doing of good and away from the doing of harm. This is not a black-and-white issue. It's probable that all work does some amount of good and some amount of harm. So it is really a question of degree.

Most people want to do work which is constructive and meaningful. So they may exaggerate the benefits of the work they're doing and ignore the harm and trouble it causes. Because of this tendency we would do well to look closely and honestly at our work. It is wise to consider the purpose of the industry, the company which employs us, the methods we use to do our jobs, and the impact of this package on the world around us. Seeing the reality of what we are doing gives us the best opportunity for choosing our life's work.

There are many criteria for choosing work including the salary, benefits, and location. Although monetary compensation provides comfort, it cannot provide meaning. Meaning comes from the work itself. It is not only a question of believing in work. It is a question of doing work which deserves such belief.

Some people may find that such considerations will mean a complete change of vocation. For others, it may mean changing jobs or employers. For still others it may mean changing the way jobs are carried out. Bringing a set of values to work-life makes occupational behavior more constructive, more meaningful, more helpful to others, and less harmful to the world which gave us life.

SUMMARY

In this chapter I have aimed to identify and interpret a brief set of guidelines for work based upon Constructive Living, life principles strongly inspired by Morita and Naikan, Japanese psychotherapies. These eight principles are:

1. Work is done for its own sake.
2. Do what needs to be done.
3. If I do not do it now, when else can I do it?
4. Pay attention.
5. Others are not controllable.
6. Do gratitude.
7. Reflect on the troubles caused others.
8. Choose constructive work.

This is not meant to be a comprehensive list. Reynolds' development of Constructive Living is rich with life wisdom, as are the traditions from which his material is drawn. I urge the reader to explore such material further. Though these principles appear simple and uncomplicated, they are often difficult to apply. We may find ourselves working in environments that do not obviously reinforce such an approach. Mastering even one of the above guidelines could have a major impact on work life. Organizations that are willing to select, train, and reward people who wish to develop these skills will reap the benefits of a better-quality work force. I began by suggesting that work is just another aspect of our lives. The people I know who are doing a good job at life are also people with whom I would want to work.

The final test of any set of life principles, inside or outside of the work setting, is whether they make sense in terms of direct life experience. Until they are applied, they remain merely ideas and words. Application gives them life.

CONSTRUCTIVE LIVING
AND REFLECTION

INTRODUCTION
TO NAIKAN

Surely at one time or another everyone has pondered why we are born. Without meaning in life we merely exist, passing through our days. But simply a philosophical discussion of life's meaning is unlikely to produce a commitment to a life purpose. And we must discover a life purpose if we are to live life well, perhaps if we are to live at all.

Naikan provides an experiential method of discovering a purpose for our existence. The Japanese creator of Naikan, Yoshimoto Ishin, went so far as to state that our purpose for living is to do Naikan. He believed Naikan to be that important.

As a form of psychotherapy Naikan counters the self centeredness and complaining of our neurotic moments with a more realistic perspective on life. I have often pointed out that I've never met a neurotic person who is filled with gratitude. Neither have you.

In this section of *Plunging Through the Clouds* we focus on the reflective aspect of Constructive Living. Built primarily around the practice of Yoshimoto's Naikan, it offers a constructive perspective on reality. Because my earlier work emphasized the action element of Constructive Living, originating in large measure from Morita therapy, this book presents a balancing heavy accent on the reflective side of Constructive Living, which comes mainly from Naikan. Naikan is easier than Morita for Westerners to misunderstand. Naikan usually evokes stronger emotional responses than Morita. The reader is advised to notice the feelings that emerge, but to avert their interference with exploring the content of the material presented below until a fuller understanding occurs.

In this careful introduction to the basis for the reflective aspect of Constructive Living, Gregg Krech offers a look at the variety of forms into which Naikan has developed in recent years. The significance of the personal implications of the study of Naikan inspires this chapter, too. What is it about Naikan that wrenches strong emotional responses from us? Can it be some recognition that while doing Naikan our hard-earned (and possibly false) self concepts are in jeopardy?   —DKR

12

THE PRACTICE OF NAIKAN

GREGG KRECH

"Man need only divert his attention from searching for the solution to external questions and pose the one, true inner question of how he should lead his life, and all the external questions will be resolved in the best possible way." —Leo Tolstoy

Naikan is a Japanese word which means "inside looking" or "introspection." It is a method of self-reflection which helps us to understand ourselves and what it means to be alive. The practice of Naikan was developed by Yoshimoto Ishin, a devout Buddhist layperson. It is based on the meditative, self-reflective practice of *mishirabe*. Though possessing ancient roots, it is only in the post-World War II period that Naikan has blossomed in Japan. More recently it has been introduced into the United States. Naikan appears to escape categorization as it becomes better known in the West. Some see it as a contemporary form of psychotherapy which, unlike much Western therapy, cultivates qualities of gratitude, humility and service to others. Some see it as a spiritual practice which opens the Naikansha (the person doing Naikan) to a realization of the true nature of life. Still others see it as a set of principles to guide us in our daily lives as we choose what to do each moment and how to act. These definitions are not mutually exclusive.

The core of Naikan, however, is the practice of Naikan. Without the practice of Naikan it remains only an attractive theory, floating above our lives like a cloud. By actually doing Naikan, we find it seeping into the way we live and a variety of spiritual or secular purposes may be achieved. My purpose in this article is to introduce readers to the practice of Naikan with very little theory or philosophy—a kind of "how to do it" essay. Though Naikan is relatively new to the United States, it is already being adapted to our culture with exercises and forms that make it more available to Americans. One danger is that such tinkering will result in the essence of Naikan practice being lost. The positive potential is that Naikan will continue to be Naikan by conforming to the needs of Westerners living in a contemporary world in the same way that water conforms to the rocks in a stream and continues to flow toward its destination. The traditional week-long Naikan intensive is already rooted in America. In recent years it has been offered annually on the East and West Coasts. The other forms and exercises discussed here will allow Westerners to explore Naikan in more accessible ways while retaining the option of doing the traditional Naikan intensive once they have tasted Naikan practice.

I have not attempted to present a comprehensive list of all the possible forms and exercises which have been developed. Rather here are presented only those forms and exercises which I have tried and found to be useful. Many of these exercises have been assigned to my students. Each person responds differently to different forms. You are invited to test them all and see what works best for you. Finally, I would like to apologize to my colleagues because of my inability to identify the source of many of these adaptations and give appropriate credit for them. Nearly all of us were introduced to Naikan by David Reynolds; however, I take responsibility for errors or misrepresentations which may be expressed in this paper.

THE BASIC PRACTICE

The basic method of Naikan revolves around three essential questions:

1. What have I received from others?

2. What have I given to others?

3. What difficulties and troubles have I caused others?

The question of troubles which *others* have caused *me* is conspicuously missing. Most of us have become quite proficient at noticing the way we have been hurt, mistreated, and troubled by the actions of others. We need no additional practice in this latter consideration, and Naikan offers us none. It is in the moment-to-moment noticing of what we receive from others and how we cause them trouble that Naikan helps us to develop new attention skills.

I shall begin my detailed description of Naikan practice with a brief discussion of the Naikan intensive, the most traditional of forms and the classic form of Japanese Naikan. Then I shall review a number of variations of Naikan which have evolved in the United States or Japan in recent years.

The Naikan Intensive

An information pamphlet for a Naikan Center in Nara, Japan begins with the following passage:

> "Knock at the door of your heart. Why don't you take the time to observe yourself, stay in a quiet place for one week and open your heart's door? As your own true form emerges, floating before your eyes, who knows what you will see?"

The one week period for a Naikan intensive is most common in Japan, although longer periods of time are sometimes scheduled. Five-day and seven-day Naikan intensives have been offered in the United States, as well. During the Naikan intensive the participants (again, called Naikansha) devote nearly every waking moment to doing Naikan reflection. They are given a small area in which to sit. This area is at least partially enclosed by screens or partitions. Traditionally, the Naikansha sit on the floor in any comfortable position using cushions. Wake up time is 5:00 or 5:30 in the morning, and the morning routine is handled quickly so that the Naikansha can be seated continuing their Naikan within twenty or thirty minutes of arising. Traditional Naikan begins with reflection on the mother's influence during the earliest years of the participant's childhood, perhaps from birth to nine years old. During this time the Naikansha are asked to consider the three core Naikan questions: What did I receive from my mother during this time? What did I give to her during this time? What troubles and worries did I cause her during this time?

The emphasis is on remembering concrete detail rather than generalities. For example, rather than remember that my mother washed my clothes for me all the time, I was encouraged to go deeper and remember the time that I played Little League Baseball and my mother woke up early to wash my uniform when an additional game was unexpectedly scheduled. Remembering specific incidents is challenging. It prevents sliding through the Naikan process with simple statements that so-and-so was loving and so-and-so was very supportive. Such abstract statements are of less value than recollections of detail.

Naikan students are encouraged to spend fifty to sixty percent of their time on the third question—what troubles and worries have I caused others? This question is most difficult because relatively little attention has been directed toward it previously. More attention has been focused on how others caused the Naikansha difficulties. Those who practice Naikan have the opportunity to see themselves through the eyes of another.

After several hours the Naikan guide (*shidosha*) comes and gives the students the opportunity to report out what they have remembered about this period of their life. This reporting (*mensetsu* or interview) resembles a type of confession. But there is no absolution offered by the guide. One of the appealing elements of Naikan is that the Naikansha are the sole judges of their behavior. There is no judgment from outside and no moral code forced upon those practicing intensive Naikan. Defenses are lowered because there is no one to defend against. Perhaps for the first time the participants are free to look openly and honestly at how they have lived their lives. The *shidosha* receiving the Naikan report simply listens with an open mind, and, when finished, asks the Naikansha to continue to reflect

on the next (usually, three-year) period. Eventually those who
do Naikan cover their entire life in relation to their mothers.
Then they start over again, this time doing Naikan reflection
on their fathers. Over the course of the week they may also do
Naikan on their spouses, siblings, children, teachers, good
friends, and others who have been important to them.

Normally, the ego-centered mind would seek activities to
distract the Naikansha from a practice so threatening to self-
esteem, but under these conditions there is little opportunity
for distraction. Meals are short and simple. Those engaged in
intensive Naikan are permitted to go to the bathroom whenever
necessary and to shower once each day or two. Otherwise, all
there is to do is reflect on their lives until bedtime at 9:00 or
9:30 P.M. The next morning the daily cycle begins again. This
routine continues for an entire week. Even as I was doing Naikan
so many things were being given to me. My meals were
prepared. My clothes were laundered. My bedding was provided.

Naikan continues until the last hour of the last day. Again
and again the participants review their lives in relation to others.
They may also be assigned the topic of lies and stealing. Unlike
the usual Naikan, the Naikansha are encouraged to look at their
lives, period by period, in order to identify instances in which,
broadly interpreted, they lied or stole things. When the week
is over and it is time to re-enter the world, what are the results
of such an extraordinary experience?

Interviews with others who have completed a week of
Naikan indicate that each person's experience has unique
elements and common threads. Nearly everyone I interviewed
left intensive Naikan with a strong sense of having been loved
and cared for. Resentment and anger toward specific individuals
had dissolved in some cases. Former Naikansha reported a
richness and vibrancy to the world around them that they had
seldom known. For some there was a sense of oneness, of
connection to the world and to others. In at least one other
instance a person's Naikan was followed by a period of depression. The feelings which arise during and after Naikan are
neither directly controllable nor of primary importance. Seeing
the reality of life is the important focus. One consistent result
of the Naikan experience is a heightened desire to repay others

for the many things received from them. The actions by which we give to others and care for the world around us transform our real feelings of love and gratitude into real behavior, simultaneously changing us and changing the world around us.

The Naikan intensive is, in fact, intense. It can be difficult emotionally and physically. The intensive practice varies somewhat among the centers in Japan (Reynolds, 1980, 1983). My initial training was at Senkobo Temple where the style and atmosphere reflect the Rinzai Zen and Jodo Shinshu training of Reverend Usami, the director of the center's activities. In the Naikan intensive there is no escape. The Naikansha come face to face with their lives; there is no way out. Other forms of Naikan allow one to do a Naikan exercise and then watch television or read a newspaper. The traditional intensive, however, allows hour-to-hour and day-to-day Naikan with minimal distractions.

Though Naikan can be painful and exhausting, it can also be beautiful and joyful. Does it seem extraordinary that an event could be both painful and beautiful at the same time? What about the birth of a baby?

Traditional Naikan (Non-Intensive)

Many of those who want to do Naikan find other forms more practical and available. Traditional Naikan may be done on a non-intensive basis. Several periods each week can be devoted to the same series of Naikan reflections. Each period should be at least one hour and should begin with Naikan on the mother as is traditional. If available, a teacher or counselor or anyone with Naikan experience can receive the individual's Naikan report during an individual session each week. The same ground can be covered as in the Naikan intensive; however I know of no person who has actually accomplished this undertaking. Many Constructive Living students are introduced to Naikan by engaging in reflection for several hours each week on important people in their lives.

Daily (Nichijo) Naikan

Daily Naikan is a simple and effective way to practice Naikan each evening. Just before going to bed the meditator spends at least thirty minutes reflecting on the day. What was received today and from whom? What was returned to others and to whom? And what troubles were caused others? Again, the individual invests at least half the time on the third question.

I often assign my students daily Naikan each evening for a week as their introduction to Naikan. Because they are reflecting on the present day it is easier to remember. They can report out their Naikan in a session at the end of the week, or they can report it out nightly as they are doing it. An example of daily Naikan is included at the end of this chapter. Variations of daily Naikan include:

1. Naikan on daily experiences as described above.

2. Daily Naikan on people whose faces you know but whose names you do not know. An example would be the bus driver who took you to the subway stop this morning.

3. Daily Naikan on people whose faces and names you do not know (An example would be the person running the subway train).

4. Daily Naikan on objects such as a car or cassette player. A friend of mine, a professional piano player, did daily Naikan on his piano.

5. Daily Naikan on forms of energy, such as electricity and heat.

6. Bedtime Naikan is another variation of daily Naikan. The Naikansha does Naikan on the day's experience while lying in bed preparing for sleep. Often it is possible to fall asleep while doing this Naikan. This method can be practiced with a partner, alternating back and forth with reports of what was received during the day. The pair continues alternate reporting until they fall asleep.

Relationship Naikan

Naikan can be an important tool for reflection on our experience with intimate partners and close friends. I have introduced Naikan to married couples who were having difficulty and contemplating divorce or separation. The purpose of Naikan is not to prevent dissolution of the marriage, but rather to help the individuals see the reality of their relationship so any decision can be based on truth rather than some illusions about themselves and their partners.

I ask individuals to do Naikan on their partners, reviewing one or two year periods, beginning with the time they first met. Those contemplating separation are encouraged to remain fully involved while they are still together. We have a Constructive Living maxim which states, "Give and give until you wave goodbye." Not doing so may result in the regret that the relationship might have been saved if more had been done. Isn't it better to be more caring and giving and loving while the opportunity is still there? Such a choice isn't necessarily easy, but its advantages may include fewer regrets later.

Naikan can be used as a prescription for troubled relationships. When problems do arise Naikan can help to view the situation from the other's perspective. However, the practice of Naikan can *prevent* certain problems and difficulties from surfacing at all. Creating rich soil is at least as important as pulling the weeds.

Naikan on Parts of the Body

Naikan may be practiced on parts of the body. For smokers Naikan reflection on the lungs may be helpful. Photographers may wish to do Naikan on their eyes. What is the reality of the contributions of these valuable parts of the body? A friend of mine had a painful toothache last month. She had to go through several days of discomfort before it could be treated and the pain subsided. What a wonderful thing it is *not* to have a toothache! How kind of the world to give us days of comfort such that the teeth go unnoticed. Perhaps it is worth taking a moment to thank your teeth for so many moments of service. What have you done for your teeth? Have you neglected them? Is there something you can do to repay them? Notice the way in which Naikan may affect the way parts of the body are treated.

Naikan Exercises

There are a number of Constructive Living exercises which are considered Naikan-like in that they support a Naikan type of awareness in our daily lives. Perhaps you will recognize the three Naikan themes upon which they are based.

1. Write thank you letters and give thank you gifts to those who serve, care and support you in concrete ways. Consciously expressing appreciation means you have to notice in detail what you are receiving from others.

2. Write apology letters to those you have caused trouble, difficulty, or harm. This exercise is more difficult than the previous one. Try picking someone with whom you're not getting along and write an apology for something you did which caused them trouble. You need not pretend that they haven't caused you trouble as well. For the moment just look at what you have done to hurt them. Notice how your mind resists doing this assignment. What can be learned from that resistance? As in all such exercises the assignment is to write the letter; mailing it is optional. There is something about the writing itself that is important.

3. Prior to each bite at mealtime silently thank one person or thing that contributed to the meal. For example, thank the farmer who grew the corn, thank the soil, thank the truck driver who delivered the corn to the store.

4. Calculate the amount of money your parents spent on you from before you were born until you turned twenty-one. Calculate this amount with as much attention to detail as possible. Then calculate how much you spent on them during that same period of time. Now do the same thing during the period of your adult life. How much have they spent on you since age twenty-one? How much have you spent on them? What is the reality of the difference between the support you have given and received?

5. Clean a drawer or closet or glove compartment. Take everything out and, as you put it back, thank each item aloud for a specific service it has given you. It might be a good idea to tell others of your exercise beforehand.

6. Perform a secret service for someone. Don't let them (or anyone else) know you did it for them. Be creative. Notice the difference in giving while knowing there will be no recognition for the deed.

7. Give something you don't use to someone who can use it. Such a gift benefits the recipient and gives new life to the item itself.

8. Garbage Naikan is an exercise in which you take a moment to thank something as you are about to throw it away. What have you received from it? How has it served you? For example, you might thank the tissue for wiping the tears from your eyes. Are there services from these objects which you have been taking for granted?

Reporting Out Naikan

Reporting out the results of self-reflection in Naikan is called "*mensetsu*," as noted above. This recounting is important, as confirmed by my own experiences and those of my students. It is better to transmit Naikan reflections to someone with personal Naikan experience. Reporting can be done by mail or by telephone, if necessary. Certified Constructive Living instructors all have some background in Naikan. Because it may not always be practical to report Naikan to a Constructive Living instructor, it may be useful to experiment with other ways of reporting. It is possible to practice Naikan with a partner and recount the recollections to each other. It is possible to recount Naikan reflections to God or Buddha or Allah or other appropriate entities. It's beneficial to report Naikan aloud.

It's not useful to report Naikan to the person who is the subject of that period of Naikan. You may wish to consider why such a practice would be unwise.

CONCLUSION

The practice of Naikan is more important than theories and talk about Naikan. Without the direct experience of doing Naikan and the Naikan-related exercises, the wisdom Naikan offers simply slips past like raindrops running off the roof of a house. But if you do your own research, if you "conduct your own experiments with Truth" (as Gandhi put it), then the insights and understanding will be your own. The wisdom based on your own experience is deeper than anything read in a book or heard on a tape.

Patricia Ryan Madson has written an account of her experience as *shidosha*, or Naikan guide, during a Naikan retreat in San Francisco. Ron and Patricia Madson are representative of the outstanding couples who practice Constructive Living and instruct others in this lifeway. It is difficult to write about Naikan in flat, cool, objective tones. The warm compassion and gratitude of the *shidosha* is apparent in this writing. —DKR

13

SHIDOSHA

PATRICIA RYAN MADSON

BACKGROUND

In December of 1989 I agreed to lead an intensive Naikan training in response to a request from several of the instructors who had completed the Constructive Living certification training that year. It was clear to me that this opportunity needed to be offered at this time. I had a week's vacation following the Christmas holidays and, upon investigation, found that rooms in the San Francisco Zen Center were also available. After checking with those interested, I announced that my husband and I would lead the seven-day retreat from January 2–9, 1990. Plans went forward, letters were exchanged, a budget was arranged, and the participants from out of state bought airline tickets to San Francisco.

Although the practice of Naikan is known and accessible in Japan today, there have been only a few opportunities to do intensive Naikan in the United States. The first of these was held in August of 1981 in San Luis Obispo. David Reynolds led eleven participants through the week of intensive Naikan, which was held in a Shinshu Buddhist church. Subsequently in 1983 Reynolds led five American participants in a second intensive, which was held at the Zen Center in Los Angeles. And a year later in 1984 a five-day intensive was arranged for two participants at the Health Center Pacific on Maui.

In March of 1989 Akira Ishii, a Japanese law professor, and his assistant, a young American Naikan enthusiast, Robert Butera, came to San Francisco to lead a seven-day intensive for four participants. I organized it and assisted at this training. It also was held at the San Francisco Zen Center on Page Street. My husband, Ronald Madson, was one of the participants. During this training, Ishii Sensei told me that I was qualified to lead an intensive on my own (perform the role of *shidosha* or guide). When he left he did so with the wish that we would carry on this work of leading Naikan in America.

THE SETTING

There were four full-time Naikansha (practitioners of Naikan) at this January, 1990 intensive—one woman and three men. They were aged from thirty-six to forty-one. In addition, there was a member of the resident Zen community, who participated part-time, doing self-reflection around his work schedule. I shall treat his case separately.

We all moved into the Zen Center on Tuesday morning, January 2, and were assigned rooms. The participants were housed, two to a room. My husband and I had a small room near them. In the space that was being shared by a man and a woman we put up a large screen to divide the room for some privacy at night. Both rooms had closets on opposite sides of the room. The closets were approximately ten inches larger than the square *zabuton* cushions used for zazen practice (roughly 40 inches square). There were airholes in the top of the door frame of the closets, and participants were free to open or close their doors to suit themselves. Even with the doors closed there was circulation of air and some light. All four Naikansha chose initially to set up their meditation cushions inside the closets.

One of the four participants was a long-time student of Zen practice. He requested permission to attend the early morning zazen sitting with the community which was held daily from 5:35-6:35 A.M. On the morning that we arrived a priest from the temple met our group and gave zazen instruction on the manners used in Zen rituals. All of the four attended this session, although only one decided to add zazen to his Naikan schedule.

It is unusual for the Zen Center to house some other meditation practice than its own. Indeed the Page Street Zen Center is officially a temple (Hoshin-ji or Beginners' Mind Temple) devoted exclusively to Zen practice. While we were renting the rooms and paying for meals at the normal guest rate, it was necessary for the governing body of the Center to sanction our presence to do Naikan there. That Naikan comes originally from a Jodo Shinshu Buddhist practice called *mishirabe*, and was last spring led by the gentle and impressive Japanese Ishii Sensei, may have been factors in persuading the community to allow us to do Naikan in their facility. Additionally, the abbot of the Zen Center, Tenshin Reb Anderson, met Ishii Sensei in March, and a deep and common respect developed between them.

The setting is ideal for Naikan in that the building is normally quiet (although the neighborhood is close to one of the worst crime areas in the city), and there is an understanding and respect for the rigors of a week-long sitting practice. This Zen group regularly does seven-day intensive meditations called *sesshin*. Additionally, they run a superb vegetarian kitchen full-time. We were able to take the prepared meals from the kitchen on trays up to the third floor and serve the participants in their rooms. This worked exceedingly well. We tried hard to minimize any confusion or disruption of the kitchen as we prepared the trays and returned the dishes.

The daily schedule began at 5:15 A.M. with the Zen community wake-up bell. This is the distinctive sound of a runner with a bell which is struck loudly and persistently. There is something of the sense of urgency about this greeting as if to say, "Life is a matter of great importance; awake without delay!" Following this signal Naikan participants were expected to rise and shower or attend to other personal needs. One participant used this early time to walk for ter. minutes in the downstairs courtyard. At 6:00 A.M. the Naikansha were instructed to be at their places doing Naikan reflection. The first interview was normally held at 7:15 A.M. just before breakfast. Lunch was at 12:30 and dinner at 6:30 P.M. All the waking hours, particularly the time from 6:00 A.M. until approximately 8:30 P.M., were designed to be devoted to Naikan reflection. Normally there were eight interviews conducted each day for each participant.

INSTRUCTION

On the day that we arrived, after quickly settling into the rooms and receiving zazen instruction, the participants and guides met for the formal introduction to the practice. I began by explaining the guidelines: they must do Naikan at all times, when bathing or eating or walking to the toilet; we recommended that the participants lower their gaze on passing others in the halls; they were to remain silent during the week except for interviews *(mensetsu)*; interviews would be conducted at approximate 90-minute intervals; all participants should begin reflecting on themselves from their mothers' perspectives for the period of the first six years of the participants' lives for the first sitting; subsequent assignments would be given by the guide following each interview; the standard three questions of Naikan were to be investigated:

1. What did I receive from this person?
2. What did I return to this person?
3. What troubles and worries did I cause this person?

I explained that if the Naikansha continued to do this practice sincerely, returning the mind again and again to these three questions, that the mind would ultimately teach itself how to do Naikan. I encouraged them to go deep and search for specific details of the past. I suggested strategies for accessing early personal memories (some of these are well known in actor training as sense or emotion memory exercises): to think of the furniture in each childhood room, to recall activities done together with mother and other family members on holidays or birthdays, to scan the mind for objects which were in their rooms, to imagine the face of the person toward whom the reflection was being pointed, and to recall items of clothing. Then I advised the participants to trace the source of these elements of their past and to direct the mind away from general reflections toward concrete detail.

I reminded them that this was a rare opportunity to do this important investigation and urged them to do their best. Following these instructions the whole group of us sat for ten minutes reflecting on all of those persons who had contributed to our being able to do this Naikan practice at this time. In other words we did Naikan on Naikan. I became acutely aware of the ongoing career efforts of David Reynolds, who has courageously introduced this practice to his students and the readers of his books in English. The Naikan lineage came to mind—from the Buddhist priests shivering and fasting in *mishirabe* to Ishin Yoshimoto, to David Reynolds, to Akira Ishii and so on to me. What a gift!

NAIKAN BEGINS

Following this meeting the silence began and the participants went back to their closets to begin formal Naikan. My husband and I were sharing responsibilities for the interviews, working around his normal eight-hour day as a construction worker. Ron would arise at 5:00 A.M. and go down to the kitchen to bring thermos bottles of hot water for tea to the rooms. He also brought fruit and cold water in pitchers. The trays with water were heavy; he walked slowly up the stairs in the darkness of morning. On the landing of the second floor was a shrine to Shunryu Suzuki Roshi with a large, very lifelike statue of him in Zen sitting posture. It is a custom in this temple on passing the shrine to stop, place hands in *gassho* and bow in respect. One of the pleasures of doing Naikan at the Zen Center was that moment when we got to stop our busy footsteps to come under the penetrating and gentle gaze of Suzuki Roshi. Ron commented once, "Did you ever notice that his statue seems to look back at you knowingly?" I had noticed that.

From the first day of Naikan sitting, the rounds of interviews began at intervals of approximately ninety minutes. This practice varied slightly around mealtimes, but never varied more than a half-hour either way. Participants reported that their subjective sense of the passage of time was unstable. Sometimes time seemed to fly by. At other times it hung heavily. Each participant's experience was, of course, unique although all were on a similar journey.

My role as *shidosha* had several functions: first, I was to care for the participants' physical welfare—looking after all of their personal and dietary needs. This enabled them to devote more of their time to the demanding practice of Naikan. It became clear to me that the manner in which I carried out this assignment was significant. My behavior and tone of voice must always show acceptance, support and concern. And secondly, I served as the one who received and guided the formal practice of Naikan. In this role it was important to listen with full attention and occasionally assist the participants in keeping their reports focused on the three questions. The guide is also available to act as a "reality check." Several participants inquired about the occurrence of hallucinations or visions. Others wanted to know if it was "normal" to sometimes fall asleep, to sometimes feel euphoric, to sometimes wonder if you are doing it right. All may be perfectly normal in this context.

After the intensive session concluded, I wrote several letters to Reynolds describing my observations of the week. I shall include some of this material here. It focuses on the participants' individual experiences. The letters of the names of the Naikansha have been changed for confidentiality.

NAIKANSHA—INDIVIDUAL DIFFERENCES

From the beginning through most of the sixth day L was in a state of deep absorption and self focus. He was in "Memory Lane." When I arrived and opened the door he would take a few minutes to slowly get himself together, to sit up and do the initial bows and exchange of information. Then he would settle into a kind of dreamy, slow storytelling mode in which he would begin recounting dozens of delightful and detailed Naikan incidents. He would make long pauses and sigh deeply as he was waiting for one of the recollections to "surface for telling." All the time (sometimes up to forty minutes and always at least twenty minutes) I sat there listening responsively. I would shift position and patiently wait until he would say, "I guess that's all."

By contrast, from the first day Y had his report together and gave it in whispered tones in three to five minutes. All week long I kept trying to figure out what was the problem with L's reporting. I reasoned that I was there to hear whatever needed to be said, and that if it took forty minutes, then that was what needed to be done. As the week went on I began to resent that he apparently had no awareness of my being there and the time he was using. Still I reasoned that I must not present a critical attitude toward the Naikansha. It wasn't that L's reporting was "wrong" because he was wasting my time; he was wasting his own time. I suddenly saw that reporting Naikan is not Naikan reflection itself. When L took forty minutes to report, he was robbing himself of the time to actually do Naikan.

On the sixth day I interrupted one of his particularly long stories to point out that it was possible and desirable to condense the information in the interview. Immediately, like a scolded child, he replied, "Oh, I see. I'm sorry. I've been wasting your time."

I replied that time was very precious. With only one day left to do Naikan, I wanted him to be able to take advantage of every minute to do Naikan. This comment apparently had the desired effect because at the next *mensetsu* review he was sitting up, ready, and had his reflections condensed. It was apparently a relief to L to hold to the form of the interview. This style of reporting allowed him to cut through some of his feeling-centered state. The correct result was awareness of the convenience of others in the present environment. So, for him, there was this one clear moment of shift. Prior to this change I had been baffled by how someone could be doing so much detailed and extensive Naikan yet wandering about and not getting the point that Naikan is discovering the convenience and perspective of others.

O did fine Naikan. Then every time O would translate the report into Zen terms. Twice she had "realizations" that, she reported, were on the magnitude and of the substance of earlier enlightenment experiences. After the Naikan, as she got on the plane, I reminded her that there was a dangerous trap in reducing the specific recollections of Naikan down to the "no eyes, no ears, no self" of Zen. All that concern with "no me" could easily let her avoid taking care of business and getting on with her service in repaying the world for herself. She reported understanding this point. We'll see what she does.

H, while doubting everything he was doing and incessantly checking to see if he was doing it right, came to some profound realizations. The best evidence for this conclusion was his voluntary suggestions about future action he needed to do: "I'm going to forgive that debt; I'm going to pay for their tickets; I'm going to do that project for free; I'm going to start working on the logistics to build a house for my parents; and so forth." Each recognition of how much he had been a "jerk" (his word) led him to some follow-up idea. I thought his Naikan was effective.

E seemed like someone who had already done a week of intensive Naikan some time in the past. She was deeply into Naikan from the start. She experienced periods of hallucinations and strong emotions. She was longing to be doing something, just as one longs for action after a week of isolated bedrest. I thought she was going to cry for joy when I gave her permission to clean the room midway through the week.

We seemed to have had a positive effect on the Zen Center community. Ron and I talked to individuals at meals. By the end of the week there appeared to be quite a bit of respect for our relentless comings and goings and ministrations. I believe there is a need for some element that offers the Naikan perspective in Zen practice, too. I sense that some of these people are "thirsty, swimming in the lake." Zen can be chilling for some.

There's one other point about doing Naikan in America which may differ significantly from doing Naikan with the Japanese. At least among the Naikansha whom I led during this intensive week there was a propensity to use the Naikan opportunity to do a sort of psychotherapy on themselves. All four Naikansha not only reported lists of what was received and given and what trouble was caused, but all went on to analyze these findings, to trace causes and effects in their lives.

> For example: "I just realized that since my father was Little League coach, scout master and head of the PTA, and since he spent literally every evening and weekend with me playing ball and scouting, then he couldn't have been spending any time alone with my mother during these years. That is probably why she seemed so distant and unhappy during my teens. I had never realized that Dad just couldn't have had any time for Mom!"

At one stage it occurred to me that a bonus that the Naikansha were getting for a week of Naikan was unique psychotherapeutic insight into their own lives. I was wary of discouraging this "putting together of the puzzle," because in all cases I thought that the resulting deductions were sound Naikan perspective and gave a kind of human psychological structure to the portfolio of "pictures" which Naikan generates. Seeing patterns of behavior and accepting responsibility for past wrongs strikes me as worthwhile.

Besides the "armchair psychoanalyzing" that everyone was doing there was another phenomenon worth reporting here. All the participants except one knew me personally and reasonably well. All had a stake in continuing to promote my good opinion of them. All, I'm sure, wanted me to think that they were doing "good Naikan." To this end they would stylize and elaborate on events to create good stories. I had the sense that it was very important to them in the first few days to demonstrate their ability to do detailed Naikan.

Each participant did Naikan reflection on his or her mother twice (in three year increments) until the present or until the time of the mother's death. During the week, everyone did Naikan reflection again on their mothers a third time at least through high school. All agreed that reflections on mothers continued to yield great bounty each time they repeated them, although nearly everyone moaned or sighed heavily on being reassigned the topic. I can distinctly remember L's "Didn't I just do my mother?"

In this chapter are examples of letters exchanged among Constructive Living instructors about their Naikan experiences. The letters are reproduced here with permission. Both the aspect of Naikan guidance (*shidosha*) and the aspect of Naikan contemplation (Naikansha) are represented. I almost used the term "recipient" for the Naikansha. But having experienced both roles of *shidosha* and Naikansha, it is clear that both are recipients. Listening to others' reflections naturally stimulates our own. Perhaps the reader of *Plunging Through the Clouds* will find this observation true, as well.   —DKR

14

CONSTRUCTIVE LIVING CORRESPONDENCE

LETTERS FROM CONSTRUCTIVE LIVING GUIDES

Following are edited excerpts from letters written by Constructive Living instructors in the midst of intensive Naikan guidance.

January 3, 1990

I have some strong sense that many of R's theoretical concerns could simply dissolve if she applies herself seriously to the week of intensive practice. And, so far, she seems to be doing so.

I am grabbing spare moments between interviews. With four participants one round of Naikan interviews takes about an hour. E is very kindly editing and condensing her material for my convenience; her deep interviews are averaging about five minutes. S has set the record for the first two days with a forty minute interview yesterday. He is averaging 25 minutes per session.

You have trained us very, very well, David. As leader of this week I owe you a tremendous debt of thanks for teaching these four participants how to do Naikan and how to value it. I see the difference clearly between those four Constructive Living instructors and the Zen student here. The Zen student's interviews have been to a great extent teaching sessions in that he is not yet doing Naikan exactly. Gently, each time I am giving specific instructions on the practice. Each session has borne fruit in small ways. The contrast between his Naikan and those who are already trained is marked at this time. He has not yet come up with a single example of something his mother gave him.

Everything is going very smoothly here at day number two. Ron has been an angel, getting up extra early to fill hot water bottles and do the wake-up call. He is available to do the first and last interview and to help with dishes, etc. We are on the third floor of the Zen Center, and the kitchen is on the first, so our knees are getting a fine workout from *seiza* kneeling and climbing the stairs.

You are one of the few persons in the world who knows what this kind of a week is like for the leader. What a privilege! What I am learning is, of course, a great, great deal. As you know I have never had children, so this becomes a very real practical experience of mothering for me. I believe that the practice of receiving Naikan teaches how to mother. My purpose is clear: to do everything possible to permit these people to be able to do Naikan and only Naikan.

Hearing Naikan is an exceptional experience from a narrative point of view. Real lives are so interesting and amazing. Of course, all four of these CL participants are exceptionally bright, articulate and intellectual so it's a particularly rich experience for me.

I remember your mentioning that Yoshimoto's knees were completely shot later in life. I heard that, but only today did I begin to understand that particular part of his sacrifice. I had imagined that the hardest part would be emotional/psychological! I am considering whether knee pain is essential to Naikan. Surely, kneeling on the floor during *mensetsu* reporting yields a reminder of intimacy and humility. Would the interview performed in two facing chairs also yield so much? Well, I may find this out, if by the end of the week what needs to be done is for me to sit in a chair. I won't resort to chairs unless I sense I'm in danger of some injury.

I find it interesting how another's Naikan triggers one's own. Someone mentioned a swing set in the back yard. I remembered one my father bought for us as a child. A word or detail of someone's experience can set off a fascinating chain of thoughts.

E is reporting and asking about the normalcy of altered states of consciousness during this practice. I assured her they are normal, and to use her Moritist understanding of the natural rise and fall of feelings and states of consciousness as solace here. Also, I suggested she make physical adjustments where possible—to change her physical position if that began to interfere, and to resist any observed tendency to analyze or psychoanalyze the material which comes up, to sit in a chair or open the door to her closet (again, some people chose to do Naikan in large closets within the rooms), to change the environment slightly.

I am experiencing a kind of guidance which seems to come through me as I lead this practice. I am following impulses that lead me to make a particular assignment or give a caution or instruction. I had earlier feared not knowing how to handle the guidance required. This is certainly as pure an experience as I have had of Reality running the show. . .using me, because there is, of course, no way that I have the training or experience which actually qualifies me to be doing this work. It seems as if one of the "many me's" is indeed someone with the understanding necessary to instruct and gently guide the participants.

Once I had an odd sensation of "being Yoshimoto." I was sitting in the *seiza* position (with legs tucked under) with my hands in fists resting on my thighs rocking back and forth in acknowledgment of what was being said. And sometimes I felt like you, making small noises of empathy deep in the throat. And sometimes I feel my ego as big as a boulder in the middle of my chest.

I have never doubted that Naikan can be my greatest teacher if I do not run from it. Well, I am certainly the benefactor here.

We are enjoying a pound of fudge sent to us by the Sapersteins. Each Naikan participant got an afternoon treat of it today.

I am convinced that Constructive Living training is a vital first step and primer for those doing intensive Naikan. Knowing that feelings come and go allows a person to hold to his purpose and stay with the Naikan rather than giving up when it gets hard. Without Moritist understanding, the spectrum of feelings which come up might appear damaging somehow. Moritist experience builds the character that permits one to do deep Naikan, I think.

I'm imagining you at your space-age computer terminal writing in the dawn. I have been happily haunted by the quote I saw next to your keyboard: "There is Reality's work that only you can do." Thank you for teaching at every moment of your life. Ron sends greetings. His steady ever present concern for others is a wonderful lesson for me.

January 11, 1990

Both Ron and I are well and looking forward to a month of "regular life" without a major workshop or commitment or speech to give. Currently my idea of a vacation is just being available to respond to what comes up.

During the Naikan intensive, I did give the reflection theme of "lies and stealing" to everyone. I qualified it by also calling it "misconduct" or "actions that the individual considered to be immoral or illegal." Two students chose to interpret this self-reflection as violations of the Buddhist precepts. Afterward, I asked each participant to comment on the value of that inquiry to them personally. All four stated independently that the lies and stealing assignment had personal value. One said that it created another lens for the same investigation—a different perspective that helped him see what he was already looking for with the three basic Naikan questions of what was received from others, what was given to others and what troubles were caused others. I believe it did good, and I heard no reports that it was inappropriate or overly moralistic. Since each person got to define for himself what "misconduct" means, it could hardly be considered an imposition. . . .

Patricia Ryan Madson

Editor's note: Patricia writes here of the Naikan assignment to examine one's past from the point of view of one's own broadly defined lying and stealing. This theme cuts across the dimension of people in one's past. When using the traditional three Naikan themes, one is invited to reflect on a particular person at a particular time in the past. When doing the lies and stealing theme, a particular time period is assigned, but no particular person.

Patricia and other Westerners have reported the lies and stealing theme to be a useful supplement to the three Naikan themes. My personal objections to this lies and stealing theme are two. My first objection is that this theme focuses only on the negative. When doing traditional Naikan my recollections of the terrible things I have done to others in the past (theme three—troubles and worries I caused others) are balanced by the recollections that others kept supporting me in spite of my misdeeds (theme one—what I received from others). So my guilt and despair are balanced by a recognition that I was cared for in spite of my imperfection. Self-esteem is supplanted by the more dependable reality esteem, if you will.

My second objection is that the three themes hold out the theoretical possibility that the Naikansha may discover that they have given to others more than they received from them. In fact, such a possibility is never realized during Naikan. And therein lies the power of Naikan, I believe. There is a chance to win, but (even using our own definitions of what was received from others and what was returned to others) we lose. When the goal from the start is to attack the self, as in the theme of lies and stealing, the impact seems to me diluted. There is no way to win that game. I prefer not to play it.

Nevertheless, I repeat that others in Japan and in the West have found the lies and stealing theme to be quite valuable. It is regularly assigned in many intensive Naikan settings in the East and in the West.

▼ ▼ ▼

LETTER FROM A PARTICIPANT

Our Naikan Intensive went very well, thanks to Patricia and Ron's considerable efforts. In retrospect I see just how feeling-centered I remain—my purpose having been to go through some remarkable experience which would change how I felt, and from that I would change my behavior. My experience was quite different. Since the week of Naikan I find myself all too aware of my continuing acts of thoughtlessness, greed, and anger. It's painfully clear that right action is doing what needs to be done based on attention paid to reality rather than from any feeling or state of mind. Feeling greedy I give.

I found Morita's principles very helpful in the Naikan experience. Naikan, too, pays attention to what I and others do and have done. The questions bypass how I felt and what I thought. In the seven days I encountered an amazing variety of mental/physical states and emotions. Again and again I would have to return to my purpose—the three questions (what was received from another, what was given to another, and what troubles were caused another). It is in this effort to attend to reality—and particularly to what I and others actually do—that I see the consonance of Naikan and Morita.

I want to thank you for your years of work bringing this practice to America. The closer I attend, the more of a beginner I find myself to be—still taming my wild and crafty mind. I look forward to helping out with the training this March in any way that I can. . . .

All of the particular memories on which I have reflected this week have brought me to one simple conclusion: Through no merit of my own, I have been given a very fortunate life in very fortunate circumstances. Across the hall is a parchment scroll on a bed of pine. "To study the Buddha Way is to study the self. To study the self is to forget the self. To forget the self is to be actualized by myriad things." Now I have some direct experience of what that means.

Gregory Willms

▼ ▼ ▼

LETTER FROM A SECOND PARTICIPANT

I have just completed seven days of intensive Naikan practice. Here are my impressions of the experience.

First of all, it was very hard work. The discipline of returning my mind to the object of meditation (the question of what someone had done for me, what I had returned, and what problems I had caused that person) was one my mind obviously did not want to face. Often, though, once my mind did start digging for the answers, a sort of momentum would build, and I was able to concentrate for long periods. There were (as I had been warned there would be) many ups and downs, and I occasionally wandered from doing Naikan "correctly." Nevertheless, my guides kept leading me back to doing the proper practice, and encouraged me to put out maximum effort.

The insights I experienced about myself and my relation to the world seemed profound at times. I also had several periods when it seemed to me that little had been achieved. The benefits, I think, will be more clearly seen in the time to come. I am sure, however, that it will be impossible for me to act with as much blind selfishness as I have many times in the past.

Michael Whiteley

▼ ▼ ▼

LETTER FROM A THIRD PARTICIPANT

Naikan has been a relentless but gentle teacher these precious, inherited moments. I walked in the garden almost every morning, but only this morning did my nose smell the first flower to greet me. One more lesson.

I have never been so carefully and constantly looked after. Even my mother took more time off than that—or did she? Go back and look again. I could say a thousand instances—but one for now, was to find a piece of chocolate fudge, just when I had been reflecting on the way my father loved me, brought me to tears.

I went through many cycles of awareness in this time. Although I am usually very healthy, the first day I was so sick

I couldn't imagine getting through at all. Time, from early on, almost disappeared and I was amazed at how one day blended into another. The markings of time were from *mensetsu* to *mensetsu*—from the gentle comings and goings. During this time I had very little appetite and was quite wakeful. I never slept through the night—was up three to four times—and yet each morning I got up refreshed and ready for the work. It was quite strange really.

My own experience of Naikan was that I was the most able to go deeply early in the morning. Walking in the garden I would cry as I remembered my parents' loving actions. It seemed that on the fourth day (I think), when I was taking a bath early in the morning, I became aware of my mother's caring and my blindness to the reality that this woman had washed every inch of me! Again, more tears.

Also, after a deep grieving over my selfishness and blindness with my parents and ex-husband, I would recover quickly. They were clean cries—and then there would be a lightness and I couldn't (wouldn't?) go back so deeply the next times. It reminds me of a quote, "Humankind cannot bear too much reality."

On the last day, Monday, I was in a very black despair. The weight of my life and how I have taken so much from people I loved, from the world, and how little I returned still seems overwhelming. I could not imagine yesterday how I could go back and go on with this history. No matter what I would do for the rest of my life, the record is quite awful—so what is the point?

I still don't know the answer to this question. The fact that people have loved and cared for me only seems to make the black blacker. But today that flower greeted me and I was able to appreciate its beauty and smell, and my Naikan guides brought more nourishing food and smiled and thanked me after they had done so much! And I am relieved and grateful to have been able to live through this Naikan experience.

Just at the end when the Naikan guides left, I saw in my mind's eye, my mother and father and I realized my birthday was coming and how much I wanted to give them something while I could. And again, the tears of recognition.

Thank you is not big enough.

Marilyn Murray

Susan Kahn wrote these responses to her intensive Naikan experience. They provide the reader with a glimpse of the new comprehension of one's personal history as provided by Naikan. Naikan leads us to the realization that forgiving our parents is trivial; Naikan is about discovering how much we need to be forgiven by our parents. It isn't pleasant to look at our past selfishness and self-centeredness, but it's vitally important to do so anyway.   —DKR

15

REFLECTIONS ON REFLECTION

SUSAN JENSEN KAHN

Some of the insights which presented themselves to me during Naikan are offered below:

It doesn't matter whether trouble and bother are intentional or not. The effects are the same.

Feeling-centered and self-centered actions may not be intentional, but have hurtful effects nonetheless.

Fathers don't give birth, but they can be hurt just as deeply as mothers.

Naikan is doing that may look, from the outside, like not doing.

We can run, but we can't hide from ourselves.

Naikan helps us outgrow our old selves, makes us want to create new selves.

Failure to act (to express gratitude, to thank, to keep in touch) can be as hurtful as acting to hurt others.

The difference between Naikan and religious confession is that we judge ourselves by our own standards. So even if we don't report everything we *know* it anyway.

In Moritist practice external reality tells us what needs doing. In Naikan practice our own standards tell us what needs doing.

Naikan makes us so sick of thinking about ourselves that we don't want to be self-centered any more.

I sometimes "misdid" myself.

The first time I did Naikan on my mother I could more or less objectively take on her perspective. The second time it was more like becoming or being her, feeling what she must have felt.

A mother feels her child's pain. The Naikansha feels the mother's pain. It's circular.

Naikan develops compassion, "suffering with."

Naikan teaches us about doing what needs to be done in spite of feelings—Mothers do this action in spite of feelings.

What mother gave and the troubles I caused her become the same sometimes. What I gave gets lost in the immensity of the other two.

I've been unaware or asleep most of my life. I want to be conscious. Stay awake!

Maintaining silence increases consciousness.

People do Naikan to stay conscious.

We need to do Naikan again and again because we need to unearth different memories each time and recode them in Naikan terms.

When doing Naikan, keep knocking at the door of memory even if there's a VACANCY sign—the sign could be wrong.

Growing up means accepting and embracing our parents, not rejecting them as some Western therapists teach.

Naikan informs us about human suffering—about which suffering is necessary and which is avoidable. And it informs us about how to avoid causing unnecessary suffering.

Cynicism seems lacking in people who have done a lot of Naikan. They say what they mean and mean what they say.

"You can only change yourself," Patricia Ryan Madson told me.

Naikan and Morita are both about attention.

Listen to everybody who is still alive.

PERSONAL EXPERIENCES WITH
CONSTRUCTIVE LIVING

My wife is a source of life instruction and inspiration. Like my parents, she lived a lot of Constructive
Living before doing any reading about it or formal
study of it. If our eyes are open we come to similar
conclusions about realistic living even while coming
from varied backgrounds. In this chapter Lynn Sanae
Reynolds offers a behind-the-scenes example of the
application of CL principles to unexpected events.
—DKR

16

JUST DOING IT

LYNN SANAE REYNOLDS

What an interesting array of options life offers! From the day
the silver anniversary issue of *Cosmopolitan* magazine (May,
1990) hit the stands, I experienced a career change, tumbling
head first into what was, for me, the unfamiliar world of an office
manager.

Lisa Interrollo's well-written article on her experiences with
Constructive Living had "reached out and touched" many
readers, and the responses were overwhelming. And David was
in Japan.

I was responsible for answering the calls and mail in Coos
Bay, referring people to the various Constructive Living
instructors near them. I soon discovered how unfamiliar I was
with the geography of our country. People were responding from
cities unknown to me. So many worries and doubts niggled as
I answered the first few calls: Would I be able to refer them to
their nearest instructor? Was the information about the
instructors current? What would I do if my computer broke
down? Where would I get a new ribbon for my printer when the
print became too light? How would I install it? Did I have enough
stationery, envelopes, stamps, brochures about books and
tapes? I worried that if I left the phone answering machine on
when I went shopping or running errands that the messages
would be garbled and I would have a difficult time trying to get

the correct information. Could I handle all the calls and mail? Would I be able to answer the callers' questions? So many questions. So many doubts.

Patricia Ryan Madson offered encouragement and support, and provided me with invaluable assistance in checking with instructors to verify phone numbers and addresses. I am deeply grateful for her help. Some of the instructors called to let me know of changed numbers or addresses, or simply to thank me for some referrals.

I bought a wall map of the United States to pinpoint the locations of the certified instructors at a glance, and a more detailed road atlas to match the city of the inquirer to the nearest instructor.

The many errands that took me away from the phone and computer were handled by tightening up my schedule, arranging stops so that trips to do the errands could be more efficiently completed. I learned which local print shop could best handle the sudden increase in stationery needs, where other supplies were easily available and most economical, where I could go to have computer problems solved, and the best time to get things done at the post office. The time-consuming tasks of folding book and tape brochures, or cutting apart stamps and sticking them on envelopes got done during "quiet time" as I watched the evening news on television.

After returning home from substitute teaching assignments several days and finding about twenty-five messages on the phone answering machine each time, (in addition to the daily stack of letters, the early morning calls I had answered before leaving for school, and the many evening and night calls after returning), I realized my mistake in underestimating the deluge of calls and mail. Turning down additional teaching assignments gave me the time to catch up on the responses. I couldn't do anything about phone messages that were cut off or callers who forgot to leave their names or addresses. After agonizing in frustration over garbled messages in which P sounded like T, S like F, B like V, then using my own discretion in spelling names and addresses, I sent replies, hoping none would return because of my mistakes.

In the mail, there were several letters with no return addresses, some with no name, several with no zip codes, some with the return addresses stamped on the envelopes, but illegibly because the ink smeared, some were illegible because the post office canceling machines covered the return addresses with the postmarks. Many were difficult to decipher simply because of illegible writing.

I have a growing respect and gratitude for the postal workers in doing their job of getting the mail to the right destination. Of several hundreds of voices I have conversed with and the additional hundreds of letters and names filed, only five letters were returned, three because of expired forwarding addresses, one person didn't leave a forwarding address, and one letter was returned without explanation.

What needed to be done was to do each task as it presented itself: answering the telephone calls as they came through, then following up with a letter to each caller; responding to each postcard or letter of inquiry as time permitted between calls; running the necessary errands as the need arose and just getting each task done one at a time. The mountain of tasks grew manageable; the seemingly impossible became routine. The panic subsided. Worries disappeared. The frustrations ironed themselves out. Meals were eaten. Replies were completed and mailed.

I have had the unique opportunity to converse with hundreds of people who are eager to learn how to "live fully" and accomplish what needs doing in their lives. Many who have not been satisfied with the therapies they have tried, wanted to know about Constructive Living. Many educators responded, asking for information to use with their students. Several college students intending to pursue careers in the mental health field wanted information for term papers or just to learn about this lifeway. Many mental health professionals responded for information about Constructive Living and training opportunities to use personally and in their professions. Most wanted to know more about living a sensible lifestyle. The following is a small sampling of responses:

"This is IT! This is LIFE! I made photocopies and distributed them to all my staff...."

"I'm so excited! This morning I got up, made a list of things to do, and did everything on it. I want to learn more!"

"I used the information this week, and it WORKS! I'm telling my friends about it...."

"I have not been so affected by anything in a very long time. I have never heard of Morita Therapy before now—though I have been in and out of therapy since my 20's (and I am now 55). I have suffered (and that's a very descriptive word) from depression for most of my life... I have tried nearly everything—self-help books, psychologists, psychiatrists, group therapy, etc. for help. Morita therapy is the most direct, honest, simple and intelligent approach to helping people that I could have ever imagined. It's wonderful... I want to know more, more, more! Morita has stirred in me the most enthusiasm I have experienced over anything in my life."

"Presently I am pursuing a Master's Degree in Counseling and would like to obtain some information on Constructive Living so that I could get involved with it for my own personal well-being and possibly incorporate the philosophy into my counseling style."

"After reading the article I was moved to write this letter... I, too, am tired of trying to dig up old feelings which must be the root of my problems. I would definitely be interested in the active approach."

"At the present moment I am seeing a therapist once every two weeks. However, I don't feel that it is moving very fast. We spend so much time discussing my past that we never quite get to the current problem."

"I am a psychiatric aide... If there is one thing that I have learned in the last ten years it is this: Traditional western psychology does not work! More often than not it leaves people worse off than before they started."

"For years I have lamented the intellectualization of therapy—finding it takes years to find out 'why,' but who cares 'why;' it doesn't help a whit today to live better."

"I received more insight in that brief article than five years of therapy."

"I have been putting into practice the three principal Morita canons. In just a week's time I feel much better about myself, others around me, and life in general. I want to continue to live like this and therefore I would like to learn more about this concept of behavior."

We have received responses from each state and nineteen foreign countries. To these kind readers we have made referrals and presented available options. I will probably never know how many or which ones followed up on the information passed through me, or whether the replies were useful and helpful to them.

Five months later, the calls and letters of inquiry continue, although fewer in number. What a fascinating variety of people with whom I have had contact. What an interesting shift in my daily purposes and priorities this practice has brought about. Life brings an amazing and varied array of choices to be made and things to be done!

Among the certified Constructive Living instructors at the end of 1990 were five physicians, eleven doctoral level psychologists, six master's level counselors, nine social workers, four registered nurses, six college professors, and nearly fifty others representing a broad spectrum of occupations. Of course, a much larger number of people had received some training in Constructive Living without achieving certification. Henry Kahn is a member of the medical profession with a sound understanding of CL theory and practice. His brief report here touches on the usefulness of this lifeway both inside and outside the medical setting.   —DKR

17

PERSONAL EXPERIENCE WITH MORITA GUIDANCE

HENRY KAHN

As a physician, I have found Morita's principles to be essential to my personal and professional life. I was introduced to Morita by David Reynolds' writings, and have continued my study through group and individual instruction with Patricia Ryan Madson. Accepting feelings, knowing my purpose, and doing what needs doing has provided my personal life with clear direction on a moment-to-moment basis. Daily difficulties of time management, commuting, partnership legal disputes, ever expanding paperwork, and weight management have all improved whenever Morita's ideas have been applied. More progress has been made in the brief period of time after my introduction to Morita than in the thirty-eight years prior.

My wife has also benefited from Morita, finding new inspiration in her art work and in her involvement in conservation issues. Our marital relationship has strengthened considerably as a side benefit of Morita practice. Greater acceptance of our emotions, and mutual support in doing what needs to be done have been evident.

As a faculty member in the Division of General Internal Medicine at the University of California, San Francisco School of Medicine, I have the opportunity to see patients, supervise nurse practitioners, and teach medical and nurse practitioner students, interns, and residents. Many patients, especially those who resemble the *shinkeishitsu* patients of Morita's time, have benefited from my recommendation to read Constructive Living books. My students and house staff have also benefited from Morita, especially when they become overwhelmed by their feelings of fear, inadequacy, or anxiety related to caring for many complicated patients. Introducing them to Morita's principles has an immediate effect in helping them do what needs doing despite their feelings. They also show long-term benefits with better coping skills when they are again faced with stressful patient encounters.

I have begun my acquaintance with the teachings of Morita. His principles have become essential to all aspects of my personal and professional life, and I am indebted to him for his insights. I am also indebted to David Reynolds for making Morita accessible to the Western world, and to Patricia Ryan Madson, Gregory Willms, and Ron Madson who have helped me toward my goal of leading a constructive life.

I well understand Henry Kahn's discovery of the usefulness of Constructive Living in medical practice. One of the reasons I shifted to full-time practice of Constructive Living was my experience teaching these principles as a faculty member at the University of Southern California School of Medicine in the early 1970's. The prescribed curriculum wasn't teaching the students some of the basic principles of everyday life—principles they needed to carry out a meaningful practice.

For example, one student came up to me after class and told of his sudden embarrassment while performing his first pelvic exam. He abruptly realized that he was touching a young woman's body in ways not ordinarily permitted a stranger. He almost fled but somehow managed to finish the exam. I advised him about the natural qualities of feelings, that they need not be controlled. I recommended that he remind himself of his purpose, that he give the best pelvic exam an embarrassed medical student ever gave a patient.

A number of such incidents helped direct me toward teaching these grammar school principles to professionals even as they do post-graduate research.

Musicians, too, can use Constructive Living in the expression of their art. Far from stifling creativity, a disciplined lifeway allows the artist to produce more work expressing that natural creativity. Music that remains unwritten or unperformed is stolen from the artist and from the public. Michael Whiteley reports on the applications of this constructive lifeway in the life of a successful professional musician.   —DKR

18

CONSTRUCTIVE LIVING—
ITS BENEFITS

MICHAEL WHITELEY

I have been practicing Constructive Living for about three years. I think that the practice of the principles has helped me a great deal in getting a realistic perspective on my life. CL has led to changes in my actions that have had a positive impact on both me and those around me. Because Constructive Living principles, which I have found to be both meaningful and true for me, emphasize changes in behavior (as opposed to changes in feelings) as being the measure of one's progress, I think the best way to evaluate the impact of Constructive Living on my life is to see how my behavior has changed in the three years since I began learning and incorporating these ideas into my life.

My home and surroundings are noticeably neater and cleaner. I am more punctual and reliable, and my time is spent more usefully than before. I indulge much less often in pursuits such as passive television viewing, reading escapist fiction, idle talk, and the like. I spend more time working, writing, cooking, and pursuing other constructive activities.

Another important change is that I now seldom drink alcohol. Although alcohol was never perceived by others as being a problem for me, since I have stopped trying to make myself "feel good" by drinking, I believe the quality of my life has improved greatly.

I have also found that my capacity for work is greater. Before Constructive Living I would usually work only when I felt like it, and would take breaks or stop working when I felt bored or tired. Now I am able to keep working despite the various feelings that come and go. I now value work as being inherently gratifying, not just as a necessary task to be done to get to the "fun things" in life.

I think that my practice of the Naikan principles has greatly helped my relationships with other people, especially those that I have had conflicts or problems with in the past. Naikan has helped me to clarify my purposes in life.

These changes in my behavior have been noticed and remarked on by several people who are close to me—they are positive, noticeable, important changes in my actions and attitudes.

In conclusion, I recommend Constructive Living to anyone seeking more satisfaction in life, as well as those with specific problems that need attention. My life has undoubtedly been altered, in a positive way, by the learning and living of the Constructive Living principles.

In 1990 the Constructive Living Center in Coos Bay sent out well over five thousand personal letters to people inquiring about CL. In addition, my private correspondence with Constructive Living students and instructors topped an additional thousand exchanges during that year. Correspondence instruction is one of the useful means by which we teach this life wisdom. Barbara Sarah's letter below provides a record of her development during the year as well as a record of her appreciation of some special people in her life.   —DKR

19

YEAR-END LETTER

BARBARA SARAH

Barbara Sarah wrote this letter at the end of 1990 and sent it to fourteen family members and friends.

Dear Friends,

This is an end-of-the-year letter to some very wonderful people who have had an important impact on my life this past year.

You have all been my teachers and for this I am truly grateful. You have taught me by your example:

how to ask for help and how to use what's offered;

how to "walk my talk;"

how to fall down and get up;

how to be with God/Reality/Truth;

how to follow my dreams;

how to continue taking risks;

how to do the work of being with another;

how to wait;

how to keep doing what's next;

how to live abundantly;

how to pay attention in every moment.

What's most important that you've all shown me—each in your own way—is how to *do* love. Either directly towards me or towards someone else in your life, you've shown me that love is action, love is doing what's right, what needs to be done. It's not about talking about it or merely saying the words, it's about. . . taking care of the dying. . . walking away when that's what's necessary. . . singing praises. . . writing letters. . . building shelves. . . crying together. . . waving from the porch. . . persistently demanding attention to proper form. . . cooking dinner. . . calling on the phone. . . shining a light in the darkness. . . getting the degree. . . showing vulnerability. . . talking over the things that are hard to talk about. . . believing in and doing the work. . . laughing together. . . staying close. . . cleaning the apartment. . . giving the shirt off your back. . . getting the job done. . . feeding the cat. . . saying no. . . changing your mind. . . saying yes. . . picnics on the beach. . . rolling up your sleeves. . . drawings on the computer. . . giving and giving until you wave goodbye.

Many of you don't know each other but you live together in the memory of what has been one of the most extraordinary, productive, meaningful, awakening, and enlightening years of my life.

Thank you all,

With appreciation,
Barbara

Jim Hutchinson is not a Constructive Living instructor. He represents the hundreds of individual students who benefit from CL every year. I suppose that any ongoing therapeutic approach can provide clinical success stories. Statistical studies are suspect for one reason or another—biases in what is evaluated, who evaluates, when the evaluation occurs, and so forth. Like many clinicians I am satisfied to let others go through the motions of providing statistical respectability. There follows an individual account of a student's encounter with Constructive Living.
—DKR

20

SOME COMMENTS ON MY EXPERIENCE WITH CONSTRUCTIVE LIVING

JIM HUTCHINSON

I find it a bit hard to describe the impact of Morita and, to a lesser extent, Naikan therapies on my life precisely because their effects are so global and yet subtle at the same time. I do identify quite strongly with both Dr. Reynolds' and Dr. Morita's descriptions of the *shinkeishitsu* neurotic type, so I suppose that through both real causal effects and the placebo effect, the therapies have been very good for my particular kinds of dysfunctional behavior. Here I emphasize the word behavior because I no longer am quite so obsessed with my feelings or my thoughts about my feelings. My focus is now on getting things done, despite the way I may be feeling or thinking about things.

I still suffer from distracting or unpleasant sensations or thoughts, but now I tend less and less to compound my suffering by feeling guilty about such feelings or by wasting time and mental energy in endless hypothetical ruminations about them. Above all, I am now better able to start all over again with a clean slate and to quickly recover if I fail at something.

I have also been struck by the extent to which focusing with full attention on doing routine but necessary household chores is capable of relieving obsessive preoccupation with various personal problems or concerns. It has, in addition, been very impressive to see just how the principle of shifting from one kind of task to another can keep me from feeling fatigue or burn-out despite my maintaining the same or even a higher overall rate of general productivity. If I were just to consider where I would eventually like to be, I think I would be disheartened and depressed. But I am much more able to take things as they come and creatively adapt to life as it really is.

I am also able to find satisfaction in the small, incremental progress and minor successes I have been able to attain. I find that behavior ironically turns out to be the tail that wags the dog of feelings, and this revelation is probably the single most useful thing I have learned from Morita therapy.

While I have not always been able to take a full course load every quarter, I have been able to return to graduate school despite feelings of extreme performance anxiety and the knowledge that I am indeed at somewhat of a comparative disadvantage vis-à-vis my fellow students in an academic environment like this one. As I am only one quarter away from graduating, my fears now center on getting a personally meaningful and socially useful job (many M.B.A. jobs are neither!), but slowly and surely I have been able to face these challenges with more optimistic attitudes and, more impor-tantly, more constructive behaviors.

I have, in addition, found Constructive Living books to be invaluable in maintaining contact with Moritist ideas even when it is not possible or convenient to participate regularly in a Moritist group or class. The books are very clearly written and presented from a practical, commonsense point of view, and replete with concrete examples rather than dry, abstract theory. I have also gotten a lot from Gregg Krech's Doing a Good Job tape, which helped me to persevere in a somewhat difficult summer job that had a lot to offer me in the long run.

HISTORICAL BACKGROUND

21

MORITA MASATAKE: THE LIFE OF THE FOUNDER OF MORITA THERAPY

DAVID K. REYNOLDS

As the Constructive Living movement gains attention, people want to know more about the founders, Morita and Yoshimoto. What kind of people were they?

Morita Masatake (his given name can also be read Shoma) was born in Fuke Village in Kochi Prefecture on the island of Shikoku on 18 January 1874. His father was a school teacher, small-business owner, and minor village official. He was strong-willed and proud. He wrote haiku poetry and fished in old age. Morita's mother married at nineteen and had a baby girl. Then she separated from her former husband and married Morita's father at age twenty-five. Remarriage has always been relatively uncommon in Japan. Morita's mother was filled with curiosity and energy. She learned to read and write as a young adult in six months. Two days after her son's birth she was up and working. In addition to housework she did cottage industry piecework, and attended classes in the arts and astronomy. She was a progressive woman for her day. Competitive, she often outdid men. She had a nervous temperament and was somewhat hypochondriacal. At age forty-three she was confined to bed with psychosomatic complaints but recovered quickly when a young child with a serious illness required her care.

Nothing went to waste in the Morita home; everything was carefully used. Even the backs of ads were used for writing. Time wasn't wasted either.

Morita grew up under the strict hand of his teacher/father. The lad disliked school, rebelling to the degree that it took seven years to complete the five year course of middle school. Morita ran away from home at least once. He suffered from various psychosomatic illnesses as a youth including headaches, stomach trouble, a disorder misdiagnosed as heart disease, and another disorder misdiagnosed as beri-beri (a vitamin deficiency found in countries where polished rice is the staple). He wet his bed until he was twelve.

As a child he was taken to a local temple. There he saw a mural depicting the tortures of hell—including lakes of fire and mountains of needles. The sensitive Morita was so upset by the possibility of facing such a future after death that he had trouble sleeping. His concern with death and insistence on the proper use of life persisted until his own death at age sixty-four in 1938.

From boyhood Morita had a broad interest in a wide variety of activities. He kept a diary from his junior high school days until a few days before his death. He cared for rabbits, carp, and monkeys, but didn't like dogs or cats. He practiced archery, the music of the samisen, Zen meditation, and Japanese chess. He was intrigued by fortune telling, legends, and superstitions. He was a strong competitor, always wanting to win. He was a popular boy, getting along well with old and young, male and female, of all ranks and occupations. Throughout his life he socially drank a surprising amount of alcohol given his active lifestyle and body weakened by typhus and other diseases.

Early promise set him on an elite course that took him, in 1898, out of the small town in rural Shikoku to urban Tokyo. His early studies at Tokyo Imperial University reflected his growing interest in the human mind. He conducted research in hypnosis, dreams, delusions and superstitions. A variety of psychosomatic complaints interfered with his studies. He was concerned with headaches, stomach complaints, and a supposed problem with his heart. He tried numerous medicines and other cures with no substantial effect.

For a period during Morita's first year in the university, his father didn't send the expected school allowance, and Morita was forced to visit a pawn shop for the first time in his life. Morita was angry at his father, suspecting that he was being taken lightly or that his father was pressuring him to return home from Tokyo. So the young man decided to quit taking medicine and literally study himself to death. He intended to cause his parents to regret their actions. He immersed himself in studies without taking particular care of his body. The results were that his psychosomatic, neurasthenic symptoms disappeared; furthermore, his grades improved. There is no doubt that this experience had a profound effect on the development of Morita's thinking about the treatment of neurosis.

By 1903, at age twenty-nine, he was lecturing at Jikei University where he would become professor and chairman of the Department of Psychiatry and Neurology. In 1919 he opened his home to treat neurotic people. That year he worked with eighteen patients in this family setting. He acknowledged the importance of his wife's assistance in this unusual practice. At first he charged nothing more than expenses for room and board. Many stories come down to us from those days.

Morita went out with his patients/students to collect the discarded vegetables from the local grocer to feed the pets. Similarly, they collected discarded wood to burn for heating the bath. It was not that Morita was miserly. As noted in an earlier section, his concern was with using things properly, fully, without waste. When he discovered that representatives of the local public bath were also collecting scrap wood Morita stopped doing it.

In 1920 Morita suffered a near-fatal illness. It provoked a soul-searching commitment to a life work. After that time his activities seemed more focused.

He continued to teach at the University. His books ranged from academic texts to best sellers. He was a popular lecturer and a charming therapist. There were times when he scolded others severely, and even a few times when he hit them. He reported in his diary that he did not do so as a therapeutic technique or in order to shock his students. Rather, he was just deeply involved in their progress, and the result emerged naturally from the situation. In that era such behavior was not exceptional, and the results were felicitous.

Morita liked to entertain and amuse. He once ate ten hardboiled eggs just to show he could do it.

Perhaps it was the year 1925 in which we can find the full flowering of Morita's method. One night he couldn't sleep well. At around three o'clock in the morning, Morita arose and began writing. He wrote that neurosis is not an illness. The more one tries to cure the obsessive problem, the more one becomes obsessed by it. This characteristic perspective tied together what Morita had been doing for a number of years. But it can't be said that Morita intended to create a novel therapy. His methods evolved naturally as he tried various techniques and observed the results. As he put it, he just kept doing this and that. In fact, he never used the term "Morita therapy" at all. That term was applied to his methods after his death.

Morita's only son died after a long illness at age twenty in 1930. Then Morita's wife died in 1935. On both occasions he cried and considered life not worth living for awhile. Morita was confined to bed with high fever on occasion during the last three years of his life. He gauged his activity on the basis of an objective measure of his health, his temperature. Active work in the garden alongside his students, or walks were possible when his temperature and strength permitted. When his fever rose he stayed in his room and wrote. When it rose higher he would read, when it rose higher he would have someone read to him. He enjoyed tasty foods and sometimes slipped away to the hospital to eat favorite dishes like curry and eggs when his diet was severely restricted at home.

Morita retired at age sixty-three, a year before he died. Near the end Morita's breathing was sometimes difficult. He carefully described the progress of his disease to his medical students, using even his dying as a tool of teaching. He was fearful of dying, and considered his fear to be natural and acceptable. He remarked that he would go out of this world as he had come into it, afraid and crying. There was no need to affect some artificial posture; Morita considered himself nothing special. And in that very consideration he was extraordinary.

22

YOSHIMOTO ISHIN: THE LIFE OF THE FOUNDER OF NAIKAN*

DAVID K. REYNOLDS

Yoshimoto Ishin was born on 25 May 1916 in Yamato Koriyama in Nara Prefecture, Japan. He was born to a devout mother and a father who sat on the village council. He had a sister, one older brother and two younger brothers. While still very small Ishin was able to memorize and quote many sutras. He didn't understand their meaning, but he was praised for his ability to memorize and recite. When Ishin was nine years old, his sister, only four years of age, died suddenly after only five days' illness. Despite his religious upbringing, the death of his sister prompted the young lad to ask himself for the first time, why are we alive? For what purpose were we born?

Yoshimoto grew to be quite familiar with Buddhist texts; he taught Buddhist principles in combination with calligraphy.

---

* Most of the information in the following short biography is drawn from my translation of Yoshimoto Ishin's *Naikan no Michi (The Way of Naikan)* and Nagashima Masahiro's article *"Naikan Totteoki no Hanashi* (Auxiliary talk about Naikan)" in Yoshimoto Ishin's edited collection *Shinzen Shingo (Before and After Faith)*, published by the Naikan Kenshusho (Naikan Training Center in Nara) in 1977 and 1985 respectively.

He was taught that sin doesn't send anyone to hell, but the underlying self centeredness does. When mental darkness is cleared by self reflection, past sins become food for further reflection and a source of gratitude. But older, wiser people kept telling Yoshimoto that knowing about fire and putting his hand in it were two different things.

As a student Yoshimoto wore traditional Japanese clothing (only 10–20% of students in that rural area were wearing Western uniforms) and sang the popular songs of the time. He graduated from Koriyama Prefectural Arts School in 1932. After a time he married Kinuko, his elder brother's wife's brother's child. His dedicated and devout wife and his mother-in-law were strong positive influences on the development of Naikan.

Yoshimoto tried for enlightenment four times. The first two times he meditated in a home and a temple using the *mishirabe* form of Shinshu Buddhism. A number of people would come every couple of hours to listen to what he had recalled about his debt to specific others in the world and to ask him if he was now headed for heaven or for hell. The lack of food, water, and sleep took its toll, and Yoshimoto gave up these first two times before achieving his goal. He remembered that his urine became thick and tea-colored from the privation.

The third time he slipped away without informing anyone that he was again about to try to achieve enlightenment. He eventually hid himself away in an isolated cave determined to stay there until he died or attained satori, enlightenment. There was immediacy to his efforts as he realized that, if the roof of the cave fell in, his life would abruptly be over. The fluttering of the bats in the cave helped keep him awake. However, his family and the villagers searched for him and finally persuaded him to come down from the mountain cave. His father tearfully asked Yoshimoto to go to the temple every day, if necessary, but stay out of the cave. The young man didn't attain satori this time, but each successive time he was able to immerse himself in the self reflection more quickly.

Following the episode in the cave Yoshimoto's father opposed his son's attempts to succeed in this *mishirabe* method. Yoshimoto even devised a lie to get out of the house to go to a fictional meeting in order to try *mishirabe* again. However, wise advisors refused to cooperate in the guidance without his father's permission. During this year Yoshimoto married and was working in a fertilizer store. His wife achieved enlightenment through *mishirabe* during this year, but the fact was kept secret from Yoshimoto's father. His wife's success spurred Yoshimoto to try *mishirabe* again, but his father's opposition was a great barrier. Both young Yoshimoto and his wife realized that satori was just an initial step and needed to be followed up with further development. The teachings of Jodo Shinshu Buddhism advised Yoshimoto to work on himself rather than trying to work on the sins of others; if his own life improved so would the lives of those around him. If he thought he was already admirable then he would make no effort to improve himself and would go to hell (already was in hell).

At last, a year later, he tried again in a detached room set aside for *mishirabe*. Knowing his intellectual grasp of the material those who guided his reflection sent two elderly men with much experience to alternate listening to Yoshimoto's self reports. These men could resist any attempts to engage them in conversation or debate. Many people, however, were outside wishing for Yoshimoto's success and encouraging him with their thoughts and prayers. Material from his past was coming up in his mind, but the meditation wasn't deepening. At last, one of the old men said that Yoshimoto should give up. Everyone was wishing him the best and suffering because of his lack of success. Yoshimoto pleaded to be allowed to continue. As the man stood up to go Yoshimoto grabbed him around the knees and cried for his help. Then he lost consciousness. When he regained his senses his head was on the *tatami* mat and the world was different. It was 8:00 P.M. November 12, 1937. He was twenty-two years old. Yoshimoto couldn't help but laugh; his drawn face became round with joy. Before this moment he was so weak from lack of sleep and food that it took two men to support him to go to the bathroom. Now he walked as though on clouds. He recognized that it was all right for him to die at any time; he had accomplished the great purpose for which humans are born. His joy was so great that he couldn't sleep that fifth night, but remained awake meditating. He noticed that

his Naikan was deepest around 3:00 or 4:00 A.M. during each
of his tries for enlightenment.

Through the years between 1936 and 1946 he developed
and refined the techniques of Naikan. The formal years given
for the founding of Naikan are, from various sources, 1939–1941.
In 1945 he first posted a public announcement of the practice
of Naikan. It was during World War II. Perhaps it was during this
period that the reading of the characters of his given name was
changed from Inobu to Ishin.

Yoshimoto took on the operation of his wife's father's
simulated leather business. Yoshimoto shifted to work in a
Koriyama factory when the Osaka store was bombed and burned
during the war. Already he had practiced his developing form
of Naikan on several hundred students in the back of his house.
He saw the Naikan way of meditation as a path to enlightenment.
As we shall see, he came to see it as enlightenment itself.

From 1945 to 1948 Yoshimoto lectured around Japan
about Naikan, but he wasn't doing Naikan and was not really
generating Naikansha students with his lectures. By 1952 the
family business had come back from destruction during the war.
There were 180 employees of the Morikawa Leather Company
in which Yoshimoto was co-director along with his father-in-law.
They had twelve branches in major cities in Japan. Prospective
employees were encouraged to do Naikan. By 1972, thanks to
the influence of Naikan on attitude and service, there were over
a hundred company stores. Yoshimoto had retired from the
business world by then.

In the latter Forties Yoshimoto was overseeing fifteen
employees during the day and at night was conducting individual Naikan interviews. He slept for only an hour or two then
caught the first train to work each morning. With this pace of
life he became ill with a lung disease at the age of thirty-four.
For five years he would take a day or two of rest whenever he
began coughing up blood. At those times the Naikansha
students would come down from the second floor where they
were meditating to his sickroom for individual *mensetsu* interviews. He saw clearly during this period that he didn't want to
be a businessman devoting himself to Naikan on the side. He
wanted to do Naikan full time.

However, there were few people who wanted to do Naikan in the late 1940s and early 1950s. Yoshimoto tried soapbox teaching in front of the local train station without success. He also tried making up small, interesting booklets for children. He printed Naikan advertisements on round *uchiwa* fans and pamphlets and gave them away. But few people came for Naikan in those days.

In 1954 Yoshimoto began his successful work in juvenile and adult prisons. There were some difficulties and delays getting the prison program underway. There was concern that Naikan was a religious practice and so would be forbidden by law in prisons. However, a statement from a senior prison official was finally obtained, and Naikan began to be practiced widely through the penal system in the late Fifties and Sixties. By 1962 about 30,000 prisoners in Japan had some Naikan experience.

Around 1968 the form of Naikan was changed from "what happened during given age periods" to the three themes (What did I receive from others? What did I return to others? What were the troubles I caused others?) and specified persons during given age periods. Thus, the modern form of Naikan didn't appear until about 1968.

Between 1957 and 1972 there were thirty radio interviews and some eighty newspaper and magazine articles about Naikan. The media coverage continued up to the death of Yoshimoto in August, 1988.

Yoshimoto had some difficulties introducing Naikan outside of Japan. He once tried translating a pamphlet titled "An Introduction to Naikan" and sent it at his own expense to 2000 penal institutions in the United States. The copies were all returned. But the success in Japan continued. Yoshimoto wrote that he believed the success could be attributed to the following four characteristics:

1. There was little talk of God's or Buddha's grace or salvation.

2. One needed no formal training to practice Naikan.

3. There were no trappings of religious ritual or apparel.

4. Naikan required only self reflection, though those who wished to could practice it for religious purposes.

In the standard style practiced at Yoshimoto's Naikan Training Center in Nara, Naikan was practiced from 5:30 in the morning until 9:00 at night. Reporting out of Naikan occurred every one and a half to two hours for approximately three to five minutes each time. Twenty percent of the time was to be devoted to the themes "What did I receive from an assigned person during an assigned time period?" and "What did I return to that person?" The remaining sixty percent of the time was to be devoted to reflection on "What troubles did I cause that person during the assigned time period?"

Yoshimoto offered these suggestions for those having trouble recalling the past:

1. If your mother had died while you were a child how would you have been specifically troubled?

2. Take your mother's point of view; how did you cause her worry and difficulty?

3. There is a difference between saying immediately "I didn't return anything to her" and first searching diligently, then saying "I didn't return anything to her."

4. Consider not only the cost of items your parents bought for you but the trouble they went to in order to get them, the times they had to return clothing, for example, that didn't fit or you didn't like.

Nagashima Masahiro wrote about life in the Naikan Center in Nara during the years of his apprenticeship there. When he mentioned to Yoshimoto that he didn't think much of one of the audio tapes of one person's Naikan experience, Yoshimoto replied, "A potato worm doesn't comprehend the size of a whale."

Mrs. Yoshimoto continued to jump to every one of her husband's requests. Yoshimoto was noted for losing and forgetting things. To Mrs. Yoshimoto fell the task of finding lost items and keeping track of the whereabouts of whatever Yoshimoto might need. Wherever he was he would call out first "Mom!" If no reply came next would come "Grandma!" Finally "Kinuko!" would let his wife know that he had been calling her for a long while. Mrs. Yoshimoto treated her husband as though he were a reincarnation of the Buddha. She chose this orientation as a result of her enlightenment experience. It was her manner to treat all those she encountered with a gentle kindness and respect.

Because he was up every morning at 3:30 Yoshimoto was well-known as a person who could take a nap quickly and deeply at any time. He had a basic trust which went beyond the ordinary. For example, he often forgot to lock up the Center at night. When scolded he would say, "If we can't welcome burglars here we can't do Naikan here." He gave out the address and phone number of the Center to prisoners freely, inviting anyone and everyone to come and do Naikan. Although his wife had some reservations about that practice, living in the Center and sometimes alone, there was never any problem because of it.

People who came to do Naikan were treated as honored guests who were doing Yoshimoto the favor of practicing Naikan. Nagashima remembers the two-week task of delivering Naikan brochures to every house in the area. No one came as a result of all that work. Thus, Nagashima, too, came to feel gratitude when people arrived to do Naikan. Yoshimoto remarked many times that Naikan was the most important thing in the world, that we were all born to do Naikan.

Those who wished to leave in the midst of their week of Naikan were encouraged to stay but were permitted to leave freely with the standing invitation to return and do Naikan again at their convenience.

Yoshimoto took no vacations. Holidays were among the busiest times at the Center; they were the time that Japanese workers could come to do Naikan. Even when Yoshimoto went to lecture at nearby institutions he wouldn't stay afterward for the traditional cup of tea. The Naikansha were waiting back at the Center. He must hurry back to do the *mensetsu* interviews.

Over the years the couple had five children (two daughters and three sons) and eighteen grandchildren. Naturally, Mrs. Yoshimoto wanted to spend time with her grandchildren. But the demands of preparing meals for her husband and the Naikansha (sometimes 35 or more of them at a time) and keeping track of who had been interviewed by whom and when required her presence at the Center every day. She joyfully prepared for the one time during summer vacation each year when her grandchildren could come visit her at the Center. But Yoshimoto reminded her, "This isn't a playground for grandchildren; don't forget it is a place to do Naikan." His single-minded dedication made a deep impression on those who knew him. Whether the Naikansha were tearful or worried that they were going crazy or concerned about hurrying home to begin repaying their social debts, Yoshimoto's advice was to continue with their Naikan. He didn't ignore their other concerns, he acknowledged them; nevertheless, the Naikan was the most important task at hand.

Yoshimoto's unaffected smiling face will remain for me the model for the face of a saint or Buddha. Some time after my week of Naikan at the Nara Center I returned to do three weeks of *mensetsu* interviews there, working closely with the founder of Naikan and his wife, observing their daily lives. They were a remarkable couple. I have been many places and met many people in my anthropological career. They stand out as uniquely enlightened human beings. I last met with Yoshimoto and his wife a little over a month before his death. He was well aware that his mind was drifting into senility. Still, his face registered that smile and his words made sense. Questions about the details of how many people were currently doing Naikan at the Center and who needed the next *mensetsu* interview he confidently referred to his wife.

Following are some of the many notable quotes from Yoshimoto Ishin:

1. Naikan is about staring fixedly at death.

2. Because you don't want to die tonight without Naikan.. . .

3. Do Naikan with attention.

4. People don't change by preaching.

5. If you want to see hell, look at your heart.

6. The most important thing we were born to do is Naikan.

7. Whatever setbacks we experience, if we develop a thankful heart through Naikan, we can turn them around.

8. Use each minute, each second, for Naikan. Attentively examine your past.

9. How is your Naikan coming? What are you considering now?

10. Intensive Naikan is the basic practice, but daily Naikan is the real thing. Those who do daily Naikan are those who know real Naikan.

11. Intensive Naikan is like power poles; daily Naikan is like the power lines stringing them together.

12. If you die now your afterlife is an extension of your current existence. So it is important to do Naikan and live with a grateful heart while you are alive.

13. To take a long time in self growth is embarrassing.

14. Before you build a tall building it is important to dig a deep foundation. Naikan is like constructing a deep foundation for human life.

15. If you want to do Naikan, even if it is in the middle of planting season, however busy you might be, come do Naikan. Easter or New Years or Sunday or a holiday or in the middle of the night, anytime, just say "I came to do Naikan."

16. Without limit, without end, single-minded Naikan. Explore yourself diligently—that is the best guidance.

17. Please, just now, set your mind to do Naikan. Let's do Naikan together.

18. Don't just listen with your ears; listen with your heart.

19. Our mothers are the representatives of all humans. How you see your mother strongly determines how you see all humans. So we examine our relationship with our mothers first and repeatedly in Naikan.

20. For what purpose were you born into this world?

21. Today is the entrance ceremony, not graduation. You are just beginning to open your ears and to observe yourself.

22. Whether you believe or not is determined each day by how you live.

23. You are fooled by your mind, which thinks there will be a tomorrow, into wasting yourself today.

24. Make a diary of the past in order to give a correct accounting of it.

25. Know yourself. Become yourself. Become your true self.

26. Doing Naikan you will be truly led to the realization of what is *your* body.

27. A bride's most important task is to do Naikan.

28. To come to your wit's end will pay off later.

29. Why should there be unchanging joy?

30. What I say today becomes me tomorrow.

31. Naikan is not a noun; it's a verb.

32. Invest 3–5 days in calculating the effects of your drinking. When, where, with whom, and how did you drink to spend that money? The companions you paid for, the side orders, gambling for drinking money, the doctors' bills for injuries from fights and for stomach and liver trouble. Then add in the loss of respect and trust of others.

33. If a person wishes to commit suicide while doing Naikan, it isn't proper Naikan.

REFERENCES

Camp, B. W. and M. A. Bash. *Think Aloud*. Champaign, IL: Research Press, 1981.

Carlson, C. L., R. G. Figueroa, & B. B. Lahey. "Behavior Therapy for Childhood Anxiety Disorders." In R. Gittelman (Ed.), *Anxiety Disorders of Childhood* (pp. 204–232). New York: Guilford Press, 1986.

Cautela, J. R. and J. Groden. *Relaxation: A Comprehensive Manual for Adults, Children, and Children With Special Needs*. Champaign, IL: Research Press, 1978.

Dinkmeyer, D. and G. D. McKay. *STEP/Teen: Systematic Training for Effective Parenting of Teens*. Circle Pines, MN: American Guidance Service, 1983.

Dobson, J. *The Strong-Willed Child*. Wheaton, IL: Tyndale House Publishers, 1987.

Fujita, Chihiro. *Morita Therapy*. New York, Tokyo: Igaku-shoin, 1986.

Ginsburg, H. and S. Opper. *Piaget's Theory of Intellectual Development, An Introduction*. Englewood Cliffs, NJ: Prentice-Hall, 1969.

Hasegawa, Yozo. "Morita-Based Self-Help Learning Groups in Japan." *International Bulletin of Morita Therapy* 1(2), 52–57, 1988.

Ilg, F. L. and L. B. Ames. *Child Behavior*. New York: Harper & Row, 1955.

Ishiyama, F. Ishu. "Shyness: Anxious Social Sensitivity and Self-Isolating Tendency." *Adolescence 19*, 903–911, 1984.

Ishiyama, F. Ishu. "Brief Morita Therapy on Social Anxiety: A Single Case Study of Therapeutic Changes." *Canadian Journal of Counselling 20*, 56–65, 1986a.

Ishiyama, F. Ishu. "Morita Therapy: Its Basic Features and Cognitive Intervention for Anxiety Treatment." *Psychotherapy 23*, 375–381, 1986b.

184   References

Ishiyama, F. Ishu. "Positive Reinterpretation of Fear of Death: A Japanese (Morita) Psychotherapy Approach to Anxiety Treatment." *Psychotherapy 23*, 556–562, 1986c.

Ishiyama, F. Ishu. "Use of Morita Therapy in Shyness Counseling in the West: Promoting Clients' Self-Acceptance and Action Taking." *Journal of Counseling and Development 65*, 547–551, 1987.

Ishiyama, F. Ishu. "Current Status of Morita Therapy Research." *International Bulletin of Morita Therapy 1*(2), 58–83, 1988.

Ishiyama, F. Ishu. "A Japanese Perspective on Client Inaction: Removing Attitudinal Blocks Through Morita Therapy." *Journal of Counseling and Development 68*, 566–570, 1990.

Klapman, J. W. "The Case for Didactic Group Psychotherapy." *Diseases of the Nervous System* 11, 35–41, 1950.

Koga, Yoshiyuki. "On Morita Therapy." *Jikei Medical Journal* 14, 73–99, 1967.

Kora, Takehisa. "An Overview of the Theory and Practice of Morita Therapy." *International Bulletin of Morita Therapy* 2(2), 70–79, 1989.

Krech, Gregg. "A Summary of Guidelines for Constructive Living Students." Unpublished, 1988.

Krumboltz, J. D. and H. B. Krumboltz. *Changing Children's Behavior*. Englewood Cliffs, NJ: Prentice-Hall, 1972.

Malamud, D. I. and S. Machover. *Toward Self-Understanding: Group Techniques in Self-Confrontation*. Springfield, IL: Charles C. Thomas, 1965.

Marsh, L. C. "Group Therapy and the Psychiatric Clinic." *Journal of Nervous and Mental Disease*, 82, 381–390, 1935.

Ohara, Kenshiro and David K. Reynolds. "Changing Methods in Morita Psychotherapy." *International Journal of Social Psychiatry* 14(4), 305–310, 1968.

Patterson, G. R. *Living With Children* (Rev. ed.). Champaign, IL: Research Press, 1976.

Reynolds, David K. *Morita Psychotherapy*. (English, Japanese, and Spanish editions) Berkeley: University of California Press, 1976.

Reynolds, David K. *The Quiet Therapies*. Honolulu: University Press of Hawaii, 1980.

Reynolds, David K. *Naikan Psychotherapy: Meditation for Self Development*. Chicago: University of Chicago Press, 1983.

Reynolds, David K. *Constructive Living*. Honolulu: University of Hawaii Press, 1984.

Reynolds, David K. *Playing Ball on Running Water*. New York: Morrow, 1984.

Reynolds, David K. *Even in Summer the Ice Doesn't Melt*. New York: Morrow, 1986.

Reynolds, David K. *Water Bears No Scars*. New York: Morrow, 1987.

Reynolds, David K. *Constructive Living for Young People*. Tokyo: Asahi, 1988.

Reynolds, David K. *Pools of Lodging for the Moon*. New York: Morrow, 1989.

Reynolds, David K. *Flowing Bridges, Quiet Waters*. Albany, NY: SUNY Press, 1989.

Reynolds, David K. *A Thousand Waves*. New York: Morrow, 1990.

Reynolds, David K. *Thirsty, Swimming in the Lake*. New York: Morrow, 1991.

Sanders, C. C. and C. Turner. *Coping: A Guide to Stress Management*. Carthage, IL: Good Apple, 1983.

Suzuki, Tomonari. "Morita Ryoho no Tachibai Kara (From the Standpoint of Morita Therapy)." *Seishin Igaku*, 9(7), 11–19, 1967.

Takeuchi, Katashi. "On Naikan (Self-Observation) Method." *Psychologia, 8*, Nr. 1–2, 1965.

Yokoyama, Keigo. "Morita Therapy and Seiza." *Psychologia* 11, 3–4, 179-184, 1968.

CONSTRUCTIVE LIVING ACTIVITIES

ABOUT THE CENTER

The Constructive Living Center is located in Coos Bay, Oregon. The mailing address is PO Box 85, Coos Bay, OR 97420 U.S.A. The telephone number is (503) 269-5591. The Center is located in a beautiful but inaccessible area on the Pacific coast with very poor transportation connections. The nearest major airport, Eugene, is small and two hours away by car. There are no trains, and bus service is infrequent. This isolation is purposeful.

The purpose of the Center, staffed by only two people, is to coordinate the activities of Constructive Living instructors around the world. At the Center we disseminate information about Constructive Living through writing, correspondence, training and lecture tours. In November, 1991 there were nearly a hundred certified Constructive Living instructors in seven countries; our mailing list of people interested in Constructive Living was over 6500; and there were fifteen books about Constructive Living in several languages with more than 100,000 copies sold altogether. As noted in the overview, articles on Constructive Living appeared in scholarly journals and in mass media such as *The New York Times, Vogue, Cosmopolitan, U.S.A. Today, Bottom Line, New Woman, The Los Angeles Times, Your Personal Best, American Health,* and *East-West Magazine* presenting adaptations of Constructive Living ideas to millions of readers around the world.

Centers for Constructive Living also exist in New York, Chicago, San Francisco, Los Angeles, Miami, Washington, D.C., Cleveland, and elsewhere. At these centers Constructive Living instruction is available through individual sessions, correspondence, group instruction, lectures and telephone guidance.

Each year we offer intensive certification training opportunities—in New York, Washington, D.C., San Francisco, Cleveland, and elsewhere. These certification courses are open to all those interested in studying Constructive Living intensively. Mental health professionals and non-professionals are welcome to apply. Trainees from Japan and other foreign countries are welcome, although the training is ordinarily completely in English. Enrollment is limited.

The certification training is residential, with students expected to assist in the preparation of meals and housekeeping chores. Special dietary needs can usually be accommodated with advance notice. Tuition for the course was $1400 in 1991; the charge for room and board *was additional*. Limited financial assistance is sometimes available. Travel and textbooks are also additional. Copied readings are included in the course fee. In 1992 the following certification training courses were offered:

San Francisco Training   March 16–25, 1992
Patricia and Ron Madson   Phone: (415) 584-0626
Center for Constructive Living
P.O. Box 460696
San Francisco, CA 94146-0696

Upstate New York Training   August 6–15, 1992
Barbara Sarah   Phone: (914) 255-3918
72 1/2 Old Ford Rd.   or (516) 482-3918
New Paltz, NY 12561

Washington D.C. Training   August 1–10, 1992
Gregg Krech   Phone: (802) 352-9018
P.O. Box 874
Middlebury, VT 05753

Cleveland Training   August 14–23, 1992
Marilyn Murray   Phone: (216) 321-0442
2889 Edgehill Rd.
Cleveland Heights, OH 44118

A quarterly newsletter for Constructive Living, *nothing special*, was available for a $15 annual subscription fee. Write to the Constructive Living Center in Coos Bay, Oregon for details of current status.

The International Association for Constructive Living (IACL) meets annually, alternating on the East and West Coasts. The IACL also offers regional meetings. The IACL is an association for those certified in Constructive Living. At the meetings there is some business conducted, but the primary function of the meetings is to share methods of instruction and conduct advanced training in Constructive Living.

Those who instruct others in Constructive Living include physicians and other professionals, but they also include non-professionals. Because CL is not psychotherapy (it is, as Morita said, a form of re-education) there is no direct connection with health insurance, hospitals, medicine, and so forth. Of course, if an illness such as schizophrenia or bipolar disorder is involved, the student is referred to an appropriate physician for medical treatment.

There are no precise statistics on the number of students who have received individual instruction in CL. At the Constructive Living Center we receive letters from students who have been helped with problems simply by reading the books and doing the life exercises written in them. Many (but not all) of the CL students would receive no psychiatric diagnosis if examined by a professional; they are clinically "normal."

CONTRIBUTORS

Perri Ardman migrated from Peoria, Illinois via New York to the farthest reaches of the Northeast United States (Maine) in 1975 where she lives in a restored 1875 farmhouse with no cats. She was certified in Constructive Living in 1987 and has a small practice conducted largely by phone with students from various places around the country. In 1991 Ms. Ardman began teaching Constructive Working and CL seminars and workshops at the University of Southern Maine. Volunteer activities include working as a crisis counselor for a local domestic violence project and the AIDS buddy program.

In 1979 Ms. Ardman co-founded The Maine Line Company, the greeting card publisher that pioneered women's humor in social expression products. In 1987 she sold the company and now serves as a consultant to companies in the gift and greeting card industry. Between 1975 and 1982 she ghost wrote and published "how to" books with such diverse collaborators as a karate champion, a baton-twirling teacher, a rape prevention expert, a psychic, and a fund-raising expert.

Jim Hutchinson was born in New Jersey in the mid-1950s, but considers himself to be a Californian because he grew up there. He studied history, economics, management, and foreign languages at Princeton, The University of California at Santa Cruz, and UCLA, where he obtained an M.B.A. in 1990. Introverted, intuitive, and hypersensitive, Jim has spent much of his life preoccupied with the problems of being imperfect and finite in a perfect and infinite universe. He is employed as a financial analyst and spreadsheet jockey. He enjoys reading, films, foreign travel, and outdoor recreation such as camping, hiking, backpacking, and skiing. He has his doubts about some of the more clannish aspects of Japanese culture, but figures that anyone who could come up with Morita therapy and sushi can't be all bad.

Henry Kahn was born in Los Angeles, California. He graduated from Pomona College with a B.A. degree in Zoology and from the University of California at San Francisco as an M.D. He was certified in Constructive Living in the San Francisco training in 1990, and he participated in a seven-day Naikan intensive in 1991. Dr. Kahn lives with his wife, Susan, in Oakland, California. He is an internist on the clinical faculty at UCSF. He is currently introducing patients, students, and colleagues to principles of Constructive Living. He is an amateur photographer and maintains a saltwater invertebrate aquarium.

Susan Jensen Kahn was born in Los Angeles, California. She graduated from the University of California at Santa Barbara in 1972 with a B.A. in painting and drawing. She later attended the Graduate School of Business at the University of San Francisco. She has worked as a graphic designer and as a financial and computer systems analyst. She was certified in Constructive Living at the San Francisco training in 1990, and she did a week of Naikan reflection in 1991. She currently lives in Oakland, California, with her husband, Henry. She is a watercolorist specializing in landscape and botanical subjects. She is also a docent at the University of California Botanical Garden in Berkeley. She enjoys learning from the children and adults who come to the garden for tours.

Gregg Krech is co-director of the ToDo Institute in Arlington, Virginia. He has conducted training in Constructive Living, Morita therapy, and Naikan for individuals and organizations in the United States and overseas. He produced the tapes *Doing a Good Job*, which describes the application of Constructive Living to the work setting, and *Naikan: Hidden Gifts Revealed*. He has studied Naikan in the United States with David Reynolds and in Japan with Usami Shue and Nagashima Masahiro.

Patricia Ryan Madson, senior lecturer in Drama at Stanford University, has been teaching acting and improvisation for over twenty years to undergraduates. She currently teaches in Stanford's Continuing Studies Program. She was the head of the Undergraduate Acting Program until 1990. She has given lectures for the National Association of Drama Therapists, the Western Psychological Association, Duke University East Asian Studies Center, and the Meaningful Life Therapy Association in Japan. On Maui in 1987 she was certified to practice Constructive Living Instruction. Since then she has maintained an active private practice, led a monthly Constructive Living group and with her husband, Ronald Madson, who is also a Certified Instructor, administered the San Francisco Center for Constructive Living. Together they have sponsored Naikan intensives in the Bay Area. She is the American Coordinator of the

Oomoto School of the Traditional Japanese Arts in Kameoka, Japan. There she studies tea ceremony and calligraphy each June.

Marilyn Murray lives in Cleveland, Ohio, where she works as a psychotherapist and school psychologist. She has recently applied Constructive Living principles to her work as a Poet in the Schools. She is a doctoral candidate in psychology and is doing research on Naikan. She was certified in Constructive Living in 1989.

Mary J. Puckett, Ph.D., is a licensed psychologist at Greenleaf Outpatient Center, P.O. Box 80338, Chattanooga, Tennessee 37411.

Barbara Sarah has a private Constructive Living practice and works as a social worker in a public high school in Great Neck, a suburb of New York City.

Rami M. Shapiro, Ph.D., is rabbi of Temple Beth Or, a Reconstructionist synagogue in Miami, Florida. An award-winning poet and essayist, Rabbi Shapiro is the author of several collections of poetry, two prayer books, and three books on spiritual growth including *This is the Path, 12 Step Recovery in a Jewish Context.* He is a certified Constructive Living instructor, conducting various seminars and workshops in Constructive Living throughout south Florida. He finds Constructive Living principles to be powerful tools with which to recover everyday spirituality that is the Jewish lifeway.

Lynn Sanae Tamashiro Reynolds was born and raised on Kauai, Hawaii. She graduated from the University of Wisconsin with a teaching credential. Immediately, she left for the warmer climate of California, where she taught in the elementary grades. She married David K. Reynolds and continued to teach in the Los Angeles Unified School District before moving to Oregon. Currently, she manages the office at the Constructive Living Center and does substitute teaching. She is a committed Christian and an avid tennis player.

Michael Whiteley was raised in the Midwest and started playing piano at age seven. He began performing popular music professionally as a soloist and with bands at age eleven. After graduating from the University of Iowa with a Music Performance degree, he moved to San Francisco where he has performed and recorded with such diverse artists as jazz saxophonist Sonny Rollins, comedian Bob Hope, new age guitarist Peter Maunu, and Bay Area Theatre Sports, an improvisational comedy group. He was the Constructive Living student of Patricia Ryan Madson. He subsequently attended the San Francisco Training in March of 1989 where he was certified as a Constructive

Living instructor. He is also a dedicated practitioner of Vipassana meditation and yoga.

Gregory Willms lives in Santa Rosa, California, where he is a licensed marriage, family, and child counselor with a private practice. He is also a certified teacher of Constructive Living, assisting in a variety of groups, workshops, and trainings.

INDEX

Acceptance, 30, 55, 56, 61, 70, 126, 153
Accomplishment, 47, 81, 99
Action-centered, 40
Action-oriented, 82, 88
Adolescence, 54, 59, 60, 62, 63
Adulthood, 6, 27, 53, 62
Affective, 79
AIDS, 69–73
Alcohol problems, 63, 78, 157, 170
Anger, 15, 39, 43, 70, 79, 113, 136
Anomie, 6
Anxiety, 3, 5, 19, 71, 78, 79, 154, 165
Apology, 18, 117
Appreciation, 6, 18, 25, 59, 65, 88–90, 98–100, 117, 160, 162
Arugamama, 30, 71, 78
Assignments, 5, 6, 7, 18, 65, 66, 67, 81, 82, 83, 88, 94, 95, 117, 124, 133–135, 148
Attention, 4, 7, 13, 14, 22, 23, 26, 29–32, 45, 51, 53, 54, 56, 65, 66, 70–73, 78–81, 94, 96–98, 102, 109, 111, 112, 117, 126, 136, 143, 158, 162, 164, 169, 180

Bedrest, 128
Bipolar disorder, 8
Boredom, 57

Buddhism, 14, 15, 17, 20, 92, 109, 121, 123, 125, 134, 173–175. See also Shinshu Buddhism, Zen
Burn-out, 165
Butera, 122

Carlson, C. L., 54
Cautela, J. R., 58
Certification, 8, 9, 118, 121, 135, 136, 138, 148, 152
Childhood, 6, 7, 18, 27, 60, 62, 112, 124
China, 95
Christianity, 15
Compassion, 120, 142
Complaints, 4, 52, 54, 57, 97, 170
Compliance, 8
Compulsions, 19
Confession, 112, 141
Confidence, 15, 23, 78
Controllable, 23, 36–40, 44, 55, 65, 70, 81, 97, 98, 102, 113
Coping, 59, 154
Correspondence, 5, 131, 160
Cosmopolitan, 3, 147
Counseling, 3, 4, 8, 15, 16, 150
Creativity, 156
Culture, 3, 31, 55, 88, 110
Cure, 7, 11, 20, 57, 172

Death, 41, 47, 70–73, 170–173, 177, 180
Delusions, 170

Dependency, 3, 37
Depression, 19, 31, 47, 66, 79,
    113, 150, 165
Desires, 12, 41, 42
Diagnoses, 8, 12, 69, 70, 71
Diary, 170, 171, 182
Dieting, 45
Dinkmeyer, D., 52
Disease, 69, 70, 170, 172, 176
Distraction, 47, 96, 113, 114
Divorce, 56, 57, 116
Dobson, J., 53
Dogen, 95

Embarrassment, 154
Emotions, 46, 55, 56, 60, 128,
    136, 153
Empathy, 133
Enlightenment, 127, 174–176,
    179
Esteem, 5, 6, 15, 135
Exercises, 6, 8, 18, 19, 21, 22,
    25, 65–67, 81, 82, 110, 117,
    119, 124

Failure, 6, 7, 12, 23, 24, 39, 40,
    43, 46, 62, 65, 141
Family, 4, 32, 69, 71, 72, 79,
    93, 124, 161, 171, 174, 176
Fantasize, 30
Father, 113, 128, 133, 138, 139,
    141, 169, 170–175
Fatigue, 165
Fear, 3, 12, 22, 32, 55, 56,
    69–71, 79, 154, 165, 172
Feeling-based, 40, 44, 45
Feeling-centered, 3, 40, 44,
    127, 141
Feeling-focused, 3, 87
Fixations, 15, 80
Forgiving, 6, 128, 140
Friends, 27, 69, 71, 72, 113,
    115, 150, 161

Frustration, 97, 148
Fujita, Chihiro, 55, 56, 80

Gambling, 182
Gandhi, 119
Gassho, 125
Ginsburg, H., 53
God, 42, 118, 161
Grandchildren, 36, 179, 180
Gratitude, 6, 7, 13, 52, 73, 89,
    90, 98, 99, 102, 104, 109,
    114, 120, 141, 149, 174, 179
Greed, 18, 136
Grief, 15, 47, 48, 70, 138
Guilt, 3, 41, 46, 100, 135, 164
Guru, 31

Haiku, 169
Hakkenkai. See Seikatsu no
    Hakkenkai
Happiness, 36, 37, 39, 45
Hasegawa, Yozo, 77, 78
Headaches, 170
HIV. See AIDS
Homework, 5, 7, 66, 67, 82, 83
Hoshin-ji, 123
Hospital, 71, 72, 171, 172
Husband, 42, 58, 121, 122,
    125, 131, 169, 179
Hypnosis, 170
Hypochondriacal, 169

Idealism, 12, 19
Immunodeficiency, 69
Impulses, 133
Independence, 18
Inferiority, 78
Insight, 3, 7, 119, 129, 137,
    141, 151, 154
Interrollo, Lisa, 147
Intimacy, 37, 79, 83, 115, 132
Introspection, 4, 109

Ishii, Akira, 18, 122, 123, 125
Ishiyama, F. Ishu, 52, 58
Iwai, Hiroshi, 84

JAMA, 3
Jealousy, 42
Jikei University, 44, 171
Jiriki, 14
Jodo Shinshu Buddhism. See
    Shinshu Buddhism
Judaism, 15

Klapman, J. W., 83
Koga, Yoshiyuki, 80, 83
Kora, Takehisa, 3, 78, 80
Koriyama, 173, 174, 176
Krumboltz, J. D., 52

Lifeway, 8, 22, 32, 34, 47, 62,
    120, 149, 152, 156
Love, 15, 25, 27, 36, 40-42,
    112-116, 138, 162

Malamud, D. I., 83
Manic-depressive disorder, 12
Maxims, 21, 22, 25
Meaningfulness, 92
Meaninglessness, 18
Medication, 3, 19, 44, 71, 153,
    154, 171
Meditation, 20, 31, 38, 114,
    122, 123, 137, 170, 175, 176
Mensetsu, 112, 118, 124, 127,
    132, 138, 176, 179, 180
Mindfulness, 30, 54
Mishirabe, 17, 109, 123, 125,
    174, 175
Morikawa Leather Company, 176
Mother, 27, 55, 58, 112, 114,
    124, 128, 129, 132, 138,
    139, 142, 169, 173, 178, 181
Music, 66, 70, 156, 170

Nagashima, Masahiro, 173,
    178, 179
Naikansha, 109-115, 122-130,
    135, 142, 176, 179, 180
Nara, 111, 173, 178, 180
Narcissistic, 7
Nature, 8, 30, 52, 76, 79, 94,
    109
Neurasthenia, 12, 19, 171
Neurosis, 7, 11-15, 20, 77, 78,
    83, 84, 171, 172
Newsletter, 75
Normal, 3, 15, 36, 96, 97, 123,
    125, 126, 133
No-self, 20
Nursing, 41, 72, 154
Nurturance, 25, 50, 58, 100

Obsessions, 11, 12, 15, 19, 22,
    77, 78, 164, 165, 172
Occupations, 31, 77, 152, 170
Ohara, Kenshiro, 80, 84
Okamoto, Tsuneo, 2
Orthodoxy, 3
Osaka, 176
Outpatients, 83
Overprotection, 25
Oversensitivity, 78

Pain, 13, 47, 48, 116, 132, 142
Panic, 11, 12, 149
Parents, 4, 6, 7, 18, 51, 53-61,
    66, 73, 98, 117, 128, 138,
    140, 142, 146, 171, 178
Patterson, G. R., 52
Perfectionism, 12, 19
Phobia, 11, 19, 30, 54, 78
Placebo, 164
Powerlessness, 97
Prison, 17, 177
Procrastination, 32, 95
Psychiatry, 4, 44, 75, 80, 150, 171

Psychodynamic, 4, 55
Psychologists, 138, 150, 152
Psychoses, 12, 19
Psychosomatic, 170, 171
Psychotherapy, 3, 4, 8, 11–17,
    29, 30, 69, 75, 83, 104, 109,
    128
Psychotic, 70

Quarreling, 11
Quill series, 21

Reality-based, 72
Referrals, 148, 151
Relationships, 3, 6, 12, 47, 48,
    53, 79, 87, 115, 116, 153,
    158, 181
Repaying, 5, 6, 113, 116, 127,
    180
Repentance, 17
Resistance, 17, 25, 87, 117
Responsibility, 4, 16, 18, 30,
    47, 57, 58, 64–66, 70,
    88–90, 94, 95, 100, 110,
    129, 147
Re-education, 16, 63, 83
Rinzai, 114
Risks, 63, 161
Rumination, 22, 164

Salvation, 177
Sanders, C. C., 58
Saperstein, Phil and Sheila, 90,
    133
Satori, 174, 175
Schizophrenia, 8, 19
Seikatsu no Hakkenkai, 77
Seiza, 132, 133
Self-centered, 3, 6, 9, 18, 20,
    53, 99, 140–142
Self-esteem, 54, 113

Selfishness, 18, 137–140
Senkobo, 114
Sesshin, 123
Shidosha, 5, 112, 120–122, 126,
    130
Shikoku, 169, 170
Shinkeishitsu, 11, 12, 15, 19,
    29, 30, 51–54, 78, 80, 83, 154,
    164
Shinky, 15, 29, 30. See also
    Shinkeishitsu
Shinshu Buddhism, 14, 17, 20,
    114, 121, 123, 174, 175
Shudankai, 77, 78, 79
Sociopathy, 19, 46
Stress, 54, 58, 59
Sufism, 15
Suicide, 182
Suzuki, Tomonari, 84, 125
Symptoms, 11, 15, 29, 30, 54,
    77–83, 171

Tales, 22, 25, 26
Taoism, 15
Tariki, 14
Thanks, 6, 7, 18, 22, 24, 26,
    34, 89, 99, 131, 135, 176
Tokyo, 44, 170, 171
Toraware, 15
Trauma, 19

Uncontrollable, 5, 30, 36–42,
    44, 70, 79
Unrealistic, 4–6, 12, 20
Usami, Shue, 114

Western culture, 3, 5, 15, 52,
    74, 75, 84, 104, 110, 135
Workplace, 86, 89, 94, 98
Worries, 3, 22, 25, 30, 66, 112,
    124, 135, 147, 149, 178

Yokoyama, Keigo, 84
Yoshimoto, Ishin, 6, 4, 14, 17,
    20, 34, 104, 109, 125, 133,
    169, 173, 174, 175, 176,
    177, 178, 179, 180

Zamora, Jesus, 90
Zazen, 122, 124
Zen, 14, 15, 20, 32, 95, 98,
    114, 121–132, 170
Zimbardo, Phillip G., 3